Your
Horoscope
2021

· · · · · · · · · · · · · · · · ·

Cancer

22 June – 22 July

igloobooks

igloobooks

Published in 2020
by Igloo Books Ltd
Cottage Farm
Sywell
NN6 0BJ
www.igloobooks.com

0820 001
2 4 6 8 10 9 7 5 3 1
ISBN 978-1-83852-317-6

Written by Belinda Campbell and Denise Evans

Cover design by Simon Parker
Edited by Bobby Newlyn-Jones

Printed and manufactured in China

CONTENTS
· · · · · · · · · · · · · · · · · ·

INTRODUCTION

. . . .

This 15-month guide has been designed and written to give
a concise and accessible insight into both the nature of your
star sign and the year ahead. Divided into two main sections,
the first section of this guide will give you an overview of your
character in order to help you understand how you think,
perceive the world and interact with others and – perhaps just
as importantly – why. You'll soon see that your zodiac sign
is not just affected by a few stars in the sky, but by planets,
elements, and a whole host of other factors, too.

The second section of this guide is made up of daily forecasts.
Use these to increase your awareness of what might appear on
your horizon so that you're better equipped to deal with the
days ahead. While this should never be used to dictate your life,
it can be useful to see how your energies might be affected or
influenced, which in turn can help you prepare for what life
might throw your way.

By the end of these 15 months, these two sections should have
given you a deeper understanding and awareness of yourself and,
in turn, the world around you. There are never any definite
certainties, but with an open mind you will find guidance for
what might be, and learn to take more control of your own
destiny.

THE CHARACTER
OF THE CRAB

Cancer is the cardinal sign that kicks off summer in the
zodiac calendar, and is also the first of the water signs.
These summery Crabs love rounding up family and friends for
a day at the beach. Creativity surrounds them, whether that
means whipping up a meal for loved ones or redecorating the
home. Cancerians saturate themselves with the latest trends in
food, fashion, art and culture. They will have had that trendy
new artist's work hanging on their walls long before anyone
else can jump on the bandwagon. Or perhaps the masterpiece
that Cancerians love most is their own, such as with artistic
Crab Frida Kahlo. Their creative juices flow constantly and
freely, and are born from a deep love and empathy.

For Cancerians, home is always where the heart is. Born in
the fourth house signifying the home and family, they are best
known for their unfailing love and caring nature. Some of the
most beloved figures in history, such as Nelson Mandela and
Diana, Princess of Wales, have been nurturing Cancerians.
These homebody Crabs will usually make more of an effort
than most to visit their family, wanting to surround themselves
in loving and supportive atmospheres. Cancerians also love
to invite people into their own home, hosting dinners, movie
nights and plenty of parties – especially in their younger
years. Friends and family should be careful of the crabby side,
however. 'It's my party and I'll cry if I want to' probably rings
true for most Cancerians. They can be overly sensitive, and are
renowned for their almighty moods. Security is what they crave,
and the need to settle their sometimes-unpredictable emotions.

THE CRAB

Tough on the outside yet vulnerable on the inside, the Crab symbolises many of the key traits associated with Cancerians. Those born under this sign have a negative polarity, which can mean that they are prone to processing thoughts and feelings internally, and may retreat into the safety of their own shells for long periods of time. Whilst their exterior may appear hard, Cancerians reveal their soft sensitivity to those who wait. A cosy and secure home life is an essential part to their happiness. Whether they prefer to live alone like the hermit crab or as part of a large family, Cancerians often need to spend quality time on their own for some peaceful self-reflection. With the love and support of family and friends, they can be coaxed from whatever sandy bay they may have decided to disappear into temporarily. The Crab is a unique balance of strength and vulnerability, which makes Cancerians treasured family members and fiercely reliable friends or partners.

THE MOON

The mother of the sky and the guardian sign of the zodiac calendar, the Moon and Cancerians share a bond of emotional influence. The Moon is the closest astronomical body to Earth, which is maybe why it feels so familiar, and why it governs homebody Cancer. There is a reassurance in being able to look up at the sky and watch the Moon's cyclical patterns, a constant quality that Cancerians are likely to find comfort in. The Moon's gravitational pull dictates Earth's tides, so any water sign will feel the influence of the Moon greatly. For Cancerians, their emotional ties to home and family are where the maternal influence of the Moon comes into effect. Cancerians are best known for their caring side, but this can turn into a worrisome nature or a tendency to smother those closest to them if they become ruled by their emotions. Both male and female Cancerians have an emotional intuition that is unparalleled, thanks to the Moon's guidance.

ELEMENTS, MODES AND POLARITIES

Each sign is made up of a unique combination of three defining groups: elements, modes and polarities. Each of these defining parts can manifest themselves in good and bad ways and none should be seen as a positive or a negative – including the polarities! Just like a jigsaw puzzle, piecing these groups together can help illuminate why each sign has certain characteristics and help us find a balance.

ELEMENTS

Fire: Dynamic and adventurous, signs with fire in them can be extroverted. Others are naturally drawn to them because of the positive light they give off, as well as their high levels of energy and confidence.

Earth: Signs with the earth element are steady and driven with their ambitions. They make for a solid friend, parent or partner due to their grounded influence and nurturing nature.

Air: The invisible element that influences each of the other elements significantly, air signs will provide much-needed perspective to others with their fair thinking, verbal skills and key ideas.

Water: Warm in the shallows and freezing as ice. This mysterious element is essential to the growth of everything around it, through its emotional depth and empathy.

MODES

Cardinal: Pioneers of the calendar, cardinal signs jump-start each season and are the energetic go-getters.

Fixed: Marking the middle of the calendar, fixed signs firmly denote and value steadiness and reliability.

Mutable: As the seasons end, the mutable signs adapt and give themselves over gladly to the promise of change.

POLARITIES

Positive: Typically extroverted, positive signs take physical action and embrace outside stimulus in their life.

Negative: Usually introverted, negative signs value emotional development and experiencing life from the inside out.

CANCER IN BRIEF

The table below shows the key attributes of Cancerians. Use it for quick reference and to understand more about this fascinating sign.

SYMBOL	RULING PLANET	MODE	ELEMENT	HOUSE
The Crab	Moon	Cardinal	Water	Fourth

COLOUR	BODY PART	POLARITY	GENDER	POLAR SIGN
White/Silver	Breasts	Negative	Feminine	Capricorn

ROMANTIC RELATIONSHIPS

. . . .

Born in the fourth house of family and home, security can be essential to Cancerians in a relationship. Not ones for living a life made up of one-night stands, even though they might try it out in their younger years, they want to find a stable and long-term relationship. Family can be hugely important to Cancerians, so they will more often than not be asking whether they see themselves having children with potential partners on the first or second date. Whilst security is crucial, this isn't always the right approach for finding love. Leaving themselves open to vulnerability is an important practice for any hard-shelled Cancerians struggling to let love in.

Love is usually felt deeply and intensely by Cancerians. Being so in tune and receptive to both their own and their partner's emotions makes them some of the most intuitive lovers in the entire zodiac calendar. Cancerians often instinctively know what others need, without them having to express it. Such is their sensitivity, Cancerians will be mindful of always pleasing their lovers. This innate ability to pick up on what others want makes them hugely desirable.

Cancerians may be able to tap into emotions to form meaningful relationships, but this also has its disadvantages. They can be prone to emotional outbursts as damaging as a burst dam, or as irritating as a leaky tap. Whilst Cancerians that don't have a handle on their emotions should try to work on this, an empathetic spouse who won't take their partner's outbursts to heart will help bring balance. A steady earth sign can complement water perfectly, forming a nurturing and mutually beneficial bond.

The cardinal aspect of Cancerians will usually make them happy to make the first move in love. They will also likely admire a fellow cardinal partner that matches their go-getter attitude.

ARIES: COMPATIBILITY 1/5

This pair shares opposite characteristics that don't always attract, sadly. A homely creature, the Cancerian may find the Arian's adventurous roaming too uncomfortable and unsettling. Conversely, the Arian will not thrive in this relationship if constricted or held back in any way by the Cancerian. However, these water and fire signs are true opposites, and therefore can stand to learn a great deal from one another. In particular, the Cancerian can teach the Arian to be more considered before acting, whilst the Arian can teach the Cancerian to be less worrisome.

TAURUS: COMPATIBILITY 5/5

Placed two positions apart on the zodiac calendar, a Cancerian and Taurean share a bond that can feel just like home. The Cancerian's frequent displays of love are deep and clear, like two names carved into a tree! The intensity of the Taurean's affection, mixed with the Cancerian's head-over-heels approach, can see these two lovers running to the altar and settling down with babies – not always in that order. Here are two signs that will do anything for each other, and will usually prefer their own little party of two.

GEMINI: COMPATIBILITY 2/5

This air and water pairing can feel too far apart personality-wise to make a good match, but the differences could actually prove to be strengthening. The Geminian is led by the mind and the Cancerian by emotion. These contrasting perspectives can lead to misunderstandings and arguments if the line of communication isn't clear. The Geminian can help the Cancerian communicate thoughts and feelings aloud rather than keeping them bottled up, while the Cancerian can provide lessons on the value of sensitivity. With so much to learn from one another, understanding and acceptance is vital to their success.

CANCER: COMPATIBILITY 4 /5

The love that two Cancerians have can run as deep and mysterious as the seas from which water signs spring. The priority of creating a strong family home will be a shared goal for these two lovers, and building a large family unit will likely bring joy and satisfaction to them both. Co-parenting is something that this nurturing pair will likely excel at. With the right amount of personal space afforded to one another, these two will be able to keep their heads above water and enjoy exploring each other's depths.

LEO: COMPATIBILITY 3/5

Leo is ruled by the Sun and Cancer by the Moon, so this pairing can feel as different as night and day. However, the Lion and the Crab can also find that they have plenty in common to form a lasting love. Born in the fourth and fifth houses that partly signify family and children, the Leonian and Cancerian share a fundamental desire to find that long-term partner to settle down with. Security is essential for the Cancerian and the fixed side of the steadfast Leonian can provide just that. This power couple could go the distance if their differences are embraced.

VIRGO: COMPATIBILITY 3/5

A practical-minded Virgoan could be the balancing force that a Cancerian needs in a partner. The Virgoan will feel loved and protected by the nurturing Cancerian, but by contrast the Cancerian can at times feel hurt by the naturally critical Virgoan. Thanks to ruling planet Mercury, the Virgoan's strong communication skills should help them patch up any problems. The earth element in Virgo and the cardinal influence in Cancer can make for a driven couple, so any loving ambitions that these two share will likely be realised together.

LIBRA: COMPATIBILITY 3/5

Ruled by the planet of love and the emotions of the Moon, the romance between a Libran and Cancerian can read like an epic poem. The Libran's love for aesthetics will be particularly attractive to the creative Crab, and encourage many artistic endeavours. The home that these two could build together might well be a thing of beauty and harmony. Both cardinal characters, the Libran and Cancerian match each other's energetic attitudes, but may fight for power in the relationship. Whilst their introvert and extrovert tendencies could clash, the Libran's search for peace could help make this relationship last.

SCORPIO: COMPATIBILITY 2/5

These two water signs could easily drown in a pool of emotion. Ruled by Mars, the Scorpian's passion for the Cancerian will be intense, and the Cancerian's feelings are highly likely to be mutual. Claws and stingers at the ready, explosive disagreements could see both sides getting hurt. Both can be stubborn and unwilling to bend in an argument, which may result in them parting ways quickly. However, once these two decide that they want to be together, they can experience a love that is unfailing in its loyalty.

SAGITTARIUS: COMPATIBILITY 1/5

A Cancerian might end up feeling lost with an adventuring wanderer that is a Sagittarian. The Sagittarian can help bring out a worldlier side to the Cancerian and show that a sense of community can stretch larger than the end of the road. With the Crab, the roaming Sagittarian can learn the benefits of settling down in a loving relationship. These two have contrasting masculine and feminine energies that can complement each other greatly, if their differences are nurtured rather than discouraged. Plenty of personal time needs to be allowed to reap the many rewards from when opposites attract.

CAPRICORN: COMPATIBILITY 5/5

Opposites on the zodiac calendar, a Capricornian and Cancerian can experience a tenacious love. Symbolised often with a fish's tail, the Sea Goat that represents the Capricornian can swim happily in the Cancerian's warm waters. The Cancerian can indeed help coax a playfulness from the Capricornian that others don't always see. The Capricornian is ruled by the authoritative planet of Saturn, so could be a strong parenting partner for the family orientated Cancerian. If these two hard workers fall in love with one another, the dedication that they share could be staggering.

AQUARIUS: COMPATIBILITY 1/5

A rebellious Aquarian and security-seeking Cancerian are not always an obvious match romantically. Whilst their core character differences may be the cause of arguments, if these two can find common interests that can cement a foundation for friendship then love could still bloom. If the Cancerian can help the intellectual Aquarian to engage emotionally, then both could mutually benefit from this unlikely but special meeting of the heart and mind. Common ground to share and foreign lands to explore will be what's needed for the Aquarian and Cancerian to find a lasting love together.

PISCES: COMPATIBILITY 4/5

These two feminine and water signs can be a vision of romance together. The Cancerian recognises the changeable river of emotion that runs within Pisces, and identifies with the alternating speeds, directions and temperatures. Here are two signs that enjoy nurturing loved ones, and so their love will be built on a mutual support system. However, the Crab and Fish need to be mindful not to get swept away by the floods of emotion they are both capable of unleashing in romantic relationships. If this is kept in check, then love and compassion can flow freely.

FAMILY AND FRIENDS

. . . .

Cancerian homes are often as warm and as comforting as a cup of tea. Born into the fourth house that represents home and family, home life is of utmost importance to these expert nest makers. Cancerians will want to make their homes an inviting environment that all the family will feel comfortable and welcome in. Capricornians make for appreciative house guests, and will be sure to notice the new artwork hanging in the artistic hallway. Cancerians who have used their creativity to decorate their own home will find that it is not wasted on aesthetic-loving Taureans, who will be full of compliments. Both Cancerians and Taureans are very much homebodies, preferring to stay in and watch a film rather than party every night, so can make highly compatible housemates.

Earth and water signs are considered to have a feminine energy and the deities associated most with the Moon are also female, so the relationships that Cancerians have with their mothers, sisters and female friends will likely help shape them greatly. Like most, the relationship with our parents plays a vital role in our overall happiness. For Cancerians, who are known for valuing family connections over most other things, this is especially applicable. Ask them to name a best friend, and they are most likely to name a parent. Cancerians likely want their own children at some stage and, if they are lucky enough to have them, will apply themselves wholeheartedly to parenting.

Cancerians are extremely intuitive beings, making them sensitive to the feelings of others. Friends and family of Cancerians might use them readily as a reliable shoulder to cry on. Cancerians are wonderful at giving loved ones reassurance and sensitive guidance, but they also expect these things in return. They can tend to dwell on the bad things that happen to them, and can hanker after constant reassurance when feeling low. When Cancerians feel like they are not receiving the sensitivity and comfort that they provide others, they can become defensive. Retreating inwards or reacting in an overly emotional manner are both typical of Cancerians that feel like they are being attacked. Their almighty moods and grudge-holding abilities can be exhausting and alienating. Peacekeeping Libran friends could help Cancerians to balance out their emotional outbursts, whilst friendly mutable Pisceans will be able to see past the mood swings. Friends, family and Cancerians themselves will do well not to dwell too readily on disagreements and practise forgiving and forgetting. The caring gestures that Cancerians are so good at showing should hopefully remedy arguments in the long run.

MONEY AND CAREERS

· · · · · · · · · · · · · · · · · ·

Being a particular star sign will not dictate certain types of career, but it can help identify potential areas for thriving in. Conversely, to succeed in the workplace, it is just as important to understand strengths and weaknesses to achieve career and financial goals.

For the Crab sign of the zodiac calendar, working in a social sector that helps to protect the vulnerable in society might be a natural calling. Whether it's working as police officers, firefighters or nurses, or other service roles, caring Cancerians thrive in a workplace where their protective instincts can be put to good use. Whether it is full-time work or a part-time passion, giving time to help others voluntarily can be an important part of their working life. Following in the footsteps of Cancerian philanthropist Diana, Princess of Wales, who was known for her kindness and charity, may be something that Cancerians wish to work towards.

Born in the fourth house that represents a love of home mixed with a Cardinal persistence, the writing profession is well suited to Cancerians. They possess the innate ability to understand emotion, and also translate it for others. Broody Cancerians should be careful of hiding away in their writing cave for too long though, as they are known for working themselves too hard. The cardinal aspect of Cancer gives this sign the driving force to leave a lasting and positive influence on the world. Seeing their words published could be a lifelong ambition for Cancerians and they may find great success, like fellow Crab Ernest Hemingway.

As with family, colleagues cannot be chosen. Therefore, it can be advantageous to use star signs to learn about their key characteristics and discover the best ways of working together. Creative and wonderfully empathetic, two Cancerians could find sharing their artistic talents an exciting collaboration. Whilst arguments could flare up, their ability to understand one another can get them back on track to working towards a shared goal.

Sea sponges for emotions, Cancerians soak up the positive and negative people in their lives, so working with the former can be essential. Optimistic Sagittarians could be just the positive colleagues to inspire less-secure Cancerians. A lack of confidence can hold this sign back professionally, so a 'fake it until you make it' attitude could do wonders for climbing the career ladder. Deep down, Cancerians are more than capable of rising to the top.

The organisational skills of the Crab are well known, and this attribute means that Cancerians are likely to succeed in their chosen career, regardless of whether they are working for someone else or managing their own business.

The satisfaction of a job well done is all this sign needs to be motivated. Money itself is generally less of a motivating factor – as long as their essential needs are provided for, Cancerians are happy to sit back slightly and spend more time with the people they love, rather than clocking up the hours in the office chasing that elusive promotion or bonus. This is certainly not to say that Cancerians lack ambition or drive, simply that they can be quite happy placing their focus on the home, once their work is sorted.

HEALTH AND WELLBEING

. . . .

Feeling things deeply, as Moon-ruled Cancerians do, means sometimes suffering from emotional insecurities and questions of self-doubt. If Cancerians find themselves sinking into anxiety, it may be that they are surrounded by too much negativity. They can be sponges for both positive and negative influences, so should review any problem areas and think how best to make improvements. A change of perspective may actually be what is required. For example, instead of wondering if they earn enough money, Cancerians should question how they can get a promotion at work. Trying to live life more fearlessly could help reduce some angst.

Spending time near water is the obvious way for Cancerians to unwind. Holidays by the coast, either home or abroad, help them to recharge their batteries and gain clarity on life. If running off to the sea isn't always feasible, taking a moment to go for a walk by a canal or pond can help them reflect on any concerns. Even a bubble bath can feel as restorative as a day at the spa.

Wellbeing practices need to be a particular priority for Cancerians. Wonderful at caring for others, they often neglect themselves. Physical exercise has been known to improve mental health and help reduce depression, and sports that lead Crabs to water, such as swimming or surfing, offer the dual benefits of both physical and emotional fitness. When exercise isn't possible, something as simple as watching a funny film could instead help lift their low moods.

HEALTH AND WELLBEING

. . . .

Having a positive influence on the world should in turn have a positive influence on philanthropic Cancerians. Volunteering for a charity, or even setting one up, could be the legacy that they take the most joy in. They should be careful of shouldering the world's problems, however, to protect their own wellbeing. In order to truly help others, Cancerians should find and regularly practise ways of releasing worries before feeling overwhelmed. Having a place of peace and serenity in the home could help them let go of whatever stresses lay outside the front door. Weekly cleaning or decluttering sessions can also help Crabs feel more at ease.

Cancer

.....

DAILY FORECASTS
for 2020

OCTOBER
· · · · · · · · · · · · · · · · · ·

Thursday 1st

Today's Full Moon in Aries shines a light on your career and legacy, as well as your current work-in-progress project. Mars, the ruler of Aries, is currently retrograde so a change is about to happen. Take a closer look now to establish what exactly needs to shift.

Friday 2nd

Your recent craving for admiration lessens as Venus moves into Virgo. You'll now want to enhance and optimise all communications, and make sure you are able to serve your neighbourhood and community. The focus is more on others than on you, which will feel deeply satisfying.

Saturday 3rd

This weekend might be the first opportunity you have to be of service to your community. It's possible that you'll invite neighbours round or you might start planning a street party. It's OK if you take on a leadership role, but just make sure you don't do everything on your own.

Sunday 4th

One thing should not be missed today and that's having some fun! Life is serious enough, and everybody enjoys a good laugh in excellent company. Be the one who makes the first step and get your friends together. Solving a mystery might also be on your to-do list, but don't overstep your boundaries, remember to respect others' feelings.

Monday 5th

Pluto, the planet of change, transformation and power, turns direct today. This means another layer of transformation has taken place and you can now start to integrate these changes. Your hard work will start to pay off, but it is not over yet.

Tuesday 6th

It's time to retreat and rest. Whenever you step back this month, it's possible that you may do so even from your family. This doesn't need to alarm you. Sometimes, it's important to simply take care of yourself and nobody else.

Wednesday 7th

Your emotions could feel intense today and there could be sudden outbursts if you don't find a way to express them consciously. If you're able to release your feelings through writing, singing, dancing or exercise, then you should be able to get through the day easily.

Thursday 8th

You still want to withdraw and are most likely not in the mood to have visitors or go out. You could possibly want to share some of your thoughts with a family member or call a close friend. Your diary would make a great companion too.

Friday 9th

Today's energy is not as easy as you, because Mars is in a strained aspect with Pluto. This is about intensity, and you could feel like you want to make a change right now. However, you do not yet have all the information needed to move ahead with your career choices. Stay patient.

Saturday 10th

You are balancing the needs of both you and your partner very easily, now. You've invested a lot to make this happen, so should feel proud that you've made it this far. A happy surprise might be on the horizon, as friends come over to visit or you receive an invitation. Be open to saying yes, the new experiences could hold wonderful rewards.

Sunday 11th

Even a tense Sun-Jupiter aspect can hold something positive. Today it will let you expand your family and home life with your partner. Perhaps you haven't been living together and decide to do so now, or there are other options that allow your bond to deepen. If you are single, it may be that you broaden your relationship with family members or close friends.

Monday 12th

What about your possessions? Do you want to get something new for your home, or do you have everything you need? If you do decide to get something, make sure it is of high value and useful at the same time - don't clutter your space with things you don't love or can't use, but it doesn't necessarily have to be a completely practical purchase. It could have a sense of luxury too.

Tuesday 13th

You could feel challenged today as you try to find harmony between home and career. You know your priorities, and you love your home, but there has to be a way to find just the right amount for both in your life. Maybe there is an opportunity in your immediate environment? Are you letting some people overstep boundaries between the two causing things to blur too much?

Wednesday 14th

Situations seem to be overly complicated sometimes, and that is especially the case when you want to find solutions to several issues at the same time. There's a deep urge for you to express more fully and to find a way to take advantage of this Mercury retrograde.

Thursday 15th

The energy may feel pretty low today, but you need to push through the day. Do not get involved in power games, especially at home or with your family. The tension will soon ease, so be the bigger person and exercise forgiveness and compassion. No-one benefits from continuing an argument unnecessarily, and making up can strengthen bonds.

Friday 16th

Happy New Moon in Libra! This event concerns your home and family, as well as your ancestors and roots in general. This would be a perfect time if you want to honour your ancestors or create a family tree. Tell your loved ones how important they are to you, it will make them happy and you will enjoy expressing yourself openly.

Saturday 17th

Today could be tricky, but also very interesting. In your contemplation about a new level of self-expression, you leave no stone unturned and search relentlessly. Be ready for some interesting revelations and ideas from your friends, listen carefully and take it on board.

Sunday 18th

Commitment is very important to you, especially in your family and relationships. Maybe you want to make further promises to your partner, or you need to negotiate some things in a new way. Take your time and but be decisive in your planning. The result should be a solid foundation and structure that you can build your future upon.

Monday 19th

There's another conflict brewing in regards to the actions, responsibilities and growth in your relationship. Your partner, or even you yourself, might fear that you are too busy with work. There could be several solutions, such as working less or working together with others in new ways.

Tuesday 20th

You suddenly want your daily life to be more exciting, so will start investigating how your social circle and friends could make it more colourful, although beware of making your relationships one-sided. If you are able to connect deeply with a particular friend, you might be able to express a wider range of your innermost self and build a really reciprocal bond.

Wednesday 21st

Venus is in a happy conversation with Pluto, so you will be able to find support in your immediate surroundings. Maybe a neighbour watches the dog or babysits the kids so that you can have some quality time to spend with your beloved. Enjoy your connection and make the most of your special time together. If you're single, spend some time pampering yourself.

Thursday 22nd

The Sun moves into Scorpio and that is always a special time
of the year. The energy draws back and becomes focused more
inwardly and intensely. Make sure you create time and space
for fun, and try not to suppress any feelings. Create an outlet
for any feelings you do have, to prevent them from bottling up
and causing you distress or exploding out at a later date.

Friday 23rd

Today is about emotional depth versus emotional distance.
It's hard for you to step back emotionally and you can become
pretty upset if somebody else seems to detach. Try not to feel
hurt, and instead consider that perhaps the other person just
uses this as a protective mechanism. You can offer support, but
remember to respect boundaries and don't interfere without
permission or invitation.

Saturday 24th

Communication is key for you in order to enhance the
foundation your relationships are built on. If you analyse
the way you communicate, you might find that there is the
potential for improvement – not only with your partner or
family, but also with your colleagues, too. Take time to learn
the languages of the people around you, in their physical
expression as well as their speech. Understanding more about
the people around you can make it easier to relate to them.

Sunday 25th

The Sun and Mercury embrace today, and you're likely to receive a deep and transformational insight. You thought you already knew the best way to express yourself and your sometimes-intense emotions, but you might come up with a brand-new outlet. Art could play a major role here - indulge your creative side. Could you start a new project, or is there an old one that you could finish or repurpose? Sometimes returning to a project with a new perspective can change your views on it, and how it turns out.

Monday 26th

The energy flows easily and connects your core as well as your heart and mind. It's a wonderful way to start the week, and all conversations might be deep and comforting at the same time. Use this flow of energy to get as much done as you can, and get a jump start on your to-do list for the week. Getting ahead can put you in a positive mood for the coming days.

Tuesday 27th

It might be time to get out your dream journal and make some notes about your dreams. They could be very powerful and insightful and hold a special message, perhaps trying to tell you something you have been unaware of about yourself. You should also check your vision board and add your newest insights and adaptions. Do these change your plans?

Wednesday 28th

Two planets move into your area of home and family. Mercury moves in retrograde motion, as if to make sure he hasn't forgotten to look at your roots and foundations. Meanwhile, Venus just moves in, ready to bring more love to your home and family. Use their influence to ensure your relationships are stable and connections are strong, and celebrate the love you have around you.

Thursday 29th

It's as though there are two hearts beating in your chest. One that seeks public recognition and success at work, and one that holds your home and family dearly and would sacrifice anything for them. Don't give up on finding a solution, there's surely some way to marry the two sides and ensure that you are professionally and personally fulfilled. You're still collecting facts right now, so don't act rashly, just compile your information and make decisions when you know more.

Friday 30th

You need to finish something at work and give it your undivided attention, but the pressure will seem to fall off as soon as the working day is over. You'll be eager to let off steam, so try to arrange some kind of post-work event with your friends.

Saturday 31st

The Full Moon in Taurus could be a bit tricky today, with lots of surprises lurking around. Elsewhere, the wonderful connections you have throughout your social circles are highlighted. Throw a Halloween party for all of your friends and be grateful for the magic you create together.

NOVEMBER

Sunday 1st

If you thought only Halloween was about trick or treat, then you're likely to be shown otherwise today. This is a day to expect the unexpected, so be prepared to change your plans and stay flexible. Remember that surprises can also be positive, so don't just be braced for the worst. Opening yourself up to new things can be beneficial to you.

Monday 2nd

Although you love to connect with friends, the time inevitably comes when you want to retreat and recharge, regain your strength emotionally and psychologically. This is normal, everyone needs some rest at times. It's not the perfect alignment when this need coincides with the start of the week. Just do your best and show up, that is enough.

Tuesday 3rd

Today, you can use the time you have on your own to come closer to a solution regarding your career and family conflict. You might have a really good idea, but it's not yet time to share it. Instead, write it down and contemplate a little more.

Wednesday 4th

Mercury retrograde is over and, by now, you should have done enough rethinking, re-evaluating and reflecting on your self-expression. You're now sure what you need in your home environment and from your family, and can start to integrate your insights into your day-to-day routines.

Thursday 5th

You should find that you can connect with your emotions easily today. You would love to follow the natural flow, but you still have some obligations and responsibilities that you must tend to. Make sure you have enough leisure time later on and use it to just follow your feelings. Taking time to do things you love is as important as ensuring all your chores and errands are completed.

Friday 6th

Remember to meet your own needs first. This is easier said than done, as you find what is expected of you from both work and your partner are demanding right now. If you can tell your partner what you want, you will get it. All you need to do is speak up, so don't be afraid. Perhaps setting clear boundaries between work and home will make it easier for you to relax and balance the two.

Saturday 7th

Self-worth and self-expression are the themes for this weekend. Tension is brewing and it could easily provoke some drama. However, this will only be a problem if you seek validation from others and place your value only on the way others perceive you. The only approval you need comes from within. Focus on self-love instead, this is far more valuable.

Sunday 8th

Let this Sunday be a day full of life and vitality. You will want to show off and be seen, so why not dress in your most daring clothes? You could maybe even start to create a play or a new art project which lets you get a little bit messy. Your inner child will thank you for bringing some fun in.

Monday 9th

You're still trying to find a way to harmonise your home and career life. Today could get you further along on this path, as you start to analyse what yin and yang sides of yourself need to be perfectly balanced out. Begin by creating a checklist, make sure that you know what you cannot compromise on, and what you might be willing to let go of to ensure you have space for everything in your life.

Tuesday 10th

Mercury is at the final degree of Libra today, which means your mental focus will sit intensely on your home and family life. You now know exactly how you want it to look. How can you achieve this? What do you need to do or change? Later on in the day, you will be ready to focus on your self-expression.

Wednesday 11th

This Wednesday is perfect for clear communication of any kind, and it can be especially helpful for having an open talk with your loved ones. Remember to listen as well as speak, as communication goes both ways, and you can't truly understand unless you are willing to hear what others have to say. Once everything is said and heard in the most objective manner, you can enjoy some cosy time together.

Thursday 12th

This is a beautiful and powerful day. You enjoy being with your family and having the protection of your home, while Jupiter and Pluto conjunct for their third and final time. This is the last deepening and expansion within your relationships, so enjoy the sensation and revel in your connections fully while you have the opportunity.

Friday 13th

There's the possibility of an issue with your family and your partner today, so be prepared for some conflict in this area. However, you and your partner will probably manage to resolve it perfectly, leaving you with a stronger bond than before. Your family are also likely to be forgiving, so no hard feelings about the matter should remain. The storm will blow over and you will all be happier on the other side.

Saturday 14th

You have been contemplating the changes necessary in your career for a long time, and now you can finally start to move forwards with your plans and take action. This is an exciting time, but don't get too carried away just yet. Mars stops its retrograde movement and turns direct, so it may take a moment before you can see change happen. Stay patient, but get yourself ready. Change is on the way, and you've been planning for this.

Sunday 15th

Happy New Moon in Scorpio! Scorpio is always connected to intensity and self-reflection. Your emotions could be stronger than usual, but this is also a perfect opportunity for you to go deeper in your feelings and start with a new creative outlet. Have you considered painting or dancing? Can you look at an older project with new eyes and transform it to reflect your new state of being?

Monday 16th

You could be tempted to escape the world by staying at home and spending time with your partner. However, there are a lot of important tasks to complete today that cannot wait. Even the most beautiful things in life ask for moderation.

Tuesday 17th

Today you could meet with friends who are able to connect some dots for you, revealing a picture that you hadn't been able to see previously. It's possible they know the right people to help get your creative outlet started. You may soon find yourself with a new group of people who share your passion.

Wednesday 18th

Be aware that your actions could lead to some difficult feelings today, so think before speaking and take a moment if you think you're getting carried away. If you become impatient or too forceful at work, your colleagues may hold it against you. Just take a deep breath and count to ten. Save the talking for tomorrow, when it will likely work out much better for you.

Thursday 19th

You will be more able to get to the root of an issue today and solve it, thanks to your amazing relationship skills. You will also be able to connect everyone together and remind them of their responsibilities. Together you can work out a structure for handling this issue, should it arise again. Working through this conflict can help strengthen your team for the future, so make sure you create the foundations for moving forwards.

Friday 20th

'Expect the unexpected' is a motto you need to take very seriously today. The energy is quite frantic and someone needs to remain level-headed. You can be that person, if you're able to detach from your feelings a little and set yourself above the chaos to remain an objective voice of reason. At least try not to add to the friction if you are unable to remove yourself in the way you need to remain unbiased.

Saturday 21st

As the Sun moves into Sagittarius, it's the time of year where you start to change things around in regards to your health and daily routine. The coolness of late autumn is blowing away any leftover summer laziness and you will want to get yourself and your home prepared for darker nights and colder days. You will want to explore different things, so you could end up cooking new and exotic dishes to integrate into your repertoire.

Sunday 22nd

Your imagination is especially vivid today, and you could find yourself orchestrating a beautiful event for your family and loved ones. There are no limits to what you can create, as the fun and joy you feel and express take priority. Don't hold back, but make sure you take the time to enjoy the spoils of your labour with your loved ones too – – they will want to share the moment with you, and you deserve your time with them. Make the moment special for everyone.

Monday 23rd

Monday morning is here again. You're focusing on your vision and have amazing ideas about how to embellish it even further. While you are high on imagination, you may want to talk about it and get others interested. This way they can support you, by making your dream come true, while keeping you grounded enough to stop you floating off on flights of unattainable fancy. Keeping your feet on the ground is important even while your head and heart are in the clouds.

Tuesday 24th

It's time to take action. You might have recently found a way to combine your work in the world with your vision and creative expression in some way. This is great news for ensuring you are creatively and professionally fulfilled. What you need to do now is carry this spark of imagination with you, as it will help you to move forwards. Don't let your enthusiasm fizzle out before you even get started.

Wednesday 25th

If you're ever in doubt about what you want to achieve, think about how you want to feel. Tune into these feelings and focus on your intuition. No-one knows you better than yourself, and if you're truly honest with yourself about what you really want and how you really feel then you cannot fail to find the right path for you. This way you will know exactly what you have to do, when to act and when to surrender.

Thursday 26th

This is likely to be a very action-packed day. It's possible that you will get a lot done and make a lot of progress, just as long as you don't get distracted by any personal conflicts that may arise. These are nothing serious, just little sensitivities and not worth getting into a long-winded lather about. You can spend your day supporting others with trivial matters and dramas, or you can spend it getting things done which can move you forwards on your path. You choose.

Friday 27th

There might be an interesting twist in today's plot. It will start as a typical working day, but then a sudden opportunity could put you in a different direction and you may find yourself in an unexpected scenario by the evening. For example, you might end up out dancing when you had planned on a night in front of the TV. See what comes your way, and be ready to say yes to invitations that you weren't anticipating.

Saturday 28th

You will want to share your creative endeavours in your social circle, whether this is something planned or spontaneous. You won't be spending the day on your own, and might meet different friends or stay with the same group throughout the day. Fantasy is always in great demand, so don't feel too restricted by reality today.

Sunday 29th

During the day, there could be important conversations leading to new opportunities in your life. Everything seems to align to ensure your maximum growth and expression, which is extremely exciting for you. After such a busy weekend, make sure you take some much-needed rest and me-time to look after yourself this evening.

Monday 30th

The month ends with a Full Moon lunar eclipse in Gemini, leaving you contemplating deeply about the year so far. You can feel the spirit of something new and exciting waiting in the wings. Create some space to reflect and write down all the important steps so far.

DECEMBER

· · · · · · · · · · · · · · · · ·

Tuesday 1st

Can you believe December is here? There's some magic in the air with the cold, and you'll feel it. With Mercury coming into your sixth house, you'll be willing and able to focus on daily business, except with a twist. You will likely change some routines and habits during that transit. The quirkier the better, work out what you need rather than what society thinks you should want or need.

Wednesday 2nd

This will most likely be a quiet day for you. You have no interest in going out to buy Christmas gifts, and hopefully all your festive parties are scheduled for later in the month and you have the day free. If you do have a function to attend, it might be an idea to make your excuses and stay home this evening, and take the time for yourself. Soul-searching should be your priority at this time.

Thursday 3rd

Make sure your needs are met at work today. You want to give your best on your projects, but others may take advantage of your strong work ethic. If you can, stand your ground and you just might earn some respect in return, which could change your working environment for the better. Pat yourself on the back, you've done a good job.

Friday 4th

You will need to take care of yourself constantly throughout today, so make sure you don't get lost in the noise of everything else which is going on. You love to support and nurture loved ones, and there will likely be a great demand for you to do so. As always, you'll try your best to make the grade. By the evening, you deserve to spoil yourself with a generous treat and some relaxation.

Saturday 5th

It's time to show up and be present! If there's a job vacancy you wish to apply for, do so. Seize the day and take the risk, you only lose out by not trying in the first place. At worst, you will remain where you are now, which isn't a bad thing, but at best you could open whole new avenues to explore. You will likely make a very good impression on the hiring managers and speak convincingly about your skills. Don't waste this opportunity and remember to be fully aware of your self-worth. You can do this job, and you will be great at it.

Sunday 6th

It sounds like a strange pursuit for a Sunday, but you should spend the day checking on your finances. With the Sun in your sixth house and the Moon in your second, it's important that you have an overview of what is coming in and what is going out, especially around this time of year. Adjustments may need to be made, so take the time to do this. You will be grateful when you go into the new year with a good plan and clear finances, so consider the future payoffs for doing your homework now.

Monday 7th

It's a great day for Christmas plans and preparations. Who will visit whom and when, what food needs to be ordered, which gifts need to be bought and wrapped. It sounds like a lot of hard work, but it will actually feel like fun. Switch on some music while you work and turn it into a party. Allow yourself to get excited about the upcoming celebrations.

Tuesday 8th

You enjoy communicating with your friends and partner, and you might even want to plan a short trip away. Ask about their preferences, but be sure to consider your own. Maybe this would make a great Christmas gift for of you to look forward to? After all, what's more valuable than time spent together?

Wednesday 9th

Is it time to put up the Christmas decorations in your home? Chances are it's one of your favourite traditions. However, be wary of taking over. Why not make an event out of it and get lots of people involved? Bake some cookies, stick some Christmassy music on, and pitch in. Let everyone help with hanging baubles and stringing up lights. Your family will truly appreciate the chance to get involved, and this is how the best memories are made.

Thursday 10th

If you're currently dealing with something that sounds too good to be true, it probably is. Be a little sceptical and suspicious and don't just walk blindly into something that appears to be a great deal but instead has downsides under the surface. There's more than meets the eye to this situation, and you'll probably get a grasp on it. Just wait and see before you jump right in.

Friday 11th

You could receive good news regarding a job application or interview. Your daily routines will need to change if you accept the position, but sometimes that is exactly what's necessary to move away from bad or outdated habits, giving yourself a clean break and a fresh new start. It's the right decision if you feel passion and excitement towards it, so consider your feelings and instincts.

Saturday 12th

Everything seems to turn out in your favour today, which will put you in a good mood. Just enjoy this Saturday, knowing that you are on the right path and moving steadily towards your ideal future. In order to welcome something new, you must let go of the old. Trust yourself and your intuition, but don't hold onto things which no longer serve you.

Sunday 13th

This will likely be a quiet Sunday. The energy is a little low and flat because there's a New Moon brewing, but that doesn't mean you have to spend the day moping. Enjoy some quiet moments and introspection instead, and take joy in a day set aside for slower, more peaceful pursuits. Maybe the magic silence of a snowy day will add to your experience.

Monday 14th

Today's New Moon in Sagittarius is potent and marks the start of a new cycle in your life. Maybe you will realise today what the future has in store for you. Make sure you consciously let go of the old and set an intention for the new. The new year is on its way, and getting yourself ready for it now means that you will be able to leap into action when it arrives.

Tuesday 15th

Who would have thought that December would be such a wonderful time for a new beginning? You're raring to start. Venus now enters your area of routine and everyday life, so she will make this even more beautiful. Quality time with your partner will also be possible today, so enjoy it with the festive magic going on around you.

Wednesday 16th

As you and your partner start to dream about your future together, you will connect on an even deeper level. Your relationship has brought much healing into your life, and by now you should know how you want to take it further. Just enjoy the love. If you're single, you could spend time making exciting plans for yourself and your family. What would you do if there was nothing at all stopping you?

Thursday 17th

Saturn leaves his home sign of Capricorn and enters Aquarius again today. Cast you mind back to what happened to you in late March, the first time Saturn assumed this position. What has changed since then? This is a time for creating new structures and foundations on which you can build your castles and futures.

Friday 18th

Another interesting and important day, as Mercury and the Sun embrace again. This event always comes with new insights and information to be revealed. In this time of new beginnings, it seems to be even more promising. The message will reveal itself over time, so make sure you are ready to receive it and act on what it tells you.

Saturday 19th

Leading up to Christmas, there is as much going on in the sky as there is down here on Earth. Jupiter is on the final day in Capricorn. He has expanded all of your relationships as far as possible and is now ready to take it all to the next level. Are you ready too?

Sunday 20th

Jupiter in Aquarius is willing to expand all your shared resources, so you could receive an influx of money during the latter half of this transit. Jupiter and Saturn conjunct, marking the beginning of a twelve year cycle that will likely anchor in a new way of life.

Monday 21st

The Sun moves in Capricorn, marking the Winter Solstice. Your focus shifts to your relationships and connections of all kinds. You will most likely spend this long night on your own. If you can, wake with the Sun. It could prove to be a magical moment.

Tuesday 22nd

Despite the impending festivities, you start to focus on work. This is highly necessary, as many matters still need to be organised or prepared. Make sure you don't push your self too far or this could end up in unpleasant discussions.

Wednesday 23rd

There might be a lot of tension today, so be sure to take plenty of breaks. Also, be especially aware of your tendency towards impulsiveness. You could easily become stressed, and it would be better if nobody gets in your way. Channel your energy into action, and be careful with tools of all kinds.

Thursday 24th

The first half of the day could still be very stressful, but thankfully the universe has good timing as the Moon comes into Taurus after midday. Everybody is able to calm down, and you should feel in the perfect mood for company. Sleep tight tonight and have sweet dreams.

Friday 25th

Merry Christmas! The Moon conjunct Uranus is usually known to reveal surprises, but today that may just mean your Christmas presents. There's still the possibility that a special guest may arrive, so welcome them with all the festive cheer you're basking in. Enjoy the time with your loved ones and your partner, and have a wonderful feast.

Saturday 26th

Today might be fairly inactive, but you still want to visit your friends and family. Instead of hot discussion, the only thing you might have to face is some stubbornness. Don't rise to it, it will dissipate if it has been ignored. Other than that, you should hopefully find that everyone is peaceful. It's perfect for a calm day and to watch a movie marathon. Perhaps take some time to enjoy the gifts you received yesterday.

Sunday 27th

It's Sunday, and you'll likely feel grateful for the opportunity of a day off from being social. Life has been full of people, conversation and food during the last few days. Stay at home and take some time for yourself, enjoy being quiet and eating good food. You need some rest and a green smoothie before you get busy again.

Monday 28th

After the peace and quiet of yesterday, life picks up the pace once more. You may be in receipt of a surprise that leaves you stunned and grateful. If all goes well, today will make you feel humble, blessed and as though everything is exactly the way it's meant to be.

Tuesday 29th

Happy Full Moon in Cancer. This is like an early New Year's Eve and a spectacular end to the year for you. Celebrate yourself today. Celebrate all the work you've done, the challenges you have faced, as well as how much you have grown and evolved. Raise a glass to all that is ahead.

Wednesday 30th

As you connect with yourself and to your vision, you intuitively realise there are old beliefs holding you back. List each one and create an action plan for how you can leave them all behind. Only then can you move fully towards your future.

Thursday 31st

That was 2020, a year that started with a bang and went on to change your life tremendously. You will grow further with your new vision, whilst also being able to work and express yourself freely. Have a happy new year, and go boldly into 2021.

Cancer

DAILY FORECASTS
for 2021

JANUARY

······················

Friday 1st

Happy New Year and welcome to 2021. A recent Full Moon in your sign illuminated all you achieved last year and it is significant. Your self-worth should be high, and you can step into this year proud and courageous. Don't be afraid to vocalise your New Year resolutions. Share a dream about travelling with a loved one.

Saturday 2nd

As the Moon is the ruler of Cancer, you're more prone to be affected by its fluctuations. Be aware of this as the year goes by and don't let it overwhelm you. Your finance and value sector is where the Moon sits today. This is good but there's also something critical in your career sector which needs your attention, so don't let other issues cause you to overlook it.

Sunday 3rd

Underneath that hard shell, you're a soft touch. You are the go-to person if messages or chores need doing. This is because you're reliable and do them so well, but don't let people take advantage of your kindness. Expect to be running around seeing to small jobs today. Maybe the sales are calling you.

Monday 4th

Communications may be problematic today as the Moon sits opposite Neptune, who likes to throw a mist over everything. Messages and travel, both long and short distance, can be affected by this. If you're unclear about how to proceed, wait until the Moon passes and you have more clarity.

Tuesday 5th

It's possible that you will have to deal with control issues.
The areas affected will be within your family and partnerships.
Mercury sits with Pluto and there can be passive-aggression
going on in important relationships. As always, you attempt to
sacrifice yourself for the sake of peace and harmony.

Wednesday 6th

Mars is spending his final day in your career sector. You must
take a good look at where your responsibilities have been
lacking lately. A last boost of effort may be needed to finish a
project to a good standard. What have you overlooked or put
aside over the festive season?

Thursday 7th

Your energy focus will be with your social groups now that
Mars has shifted. There may be a lot of invitations coming in.
Mars can help you with innovative ways to get together with
friends. Dinner engagements can be fun, but active arranged
events can be better. Get your diary out.

Friday 8th

The Moon squares off with Mercury today. This means that you
may have a heart-versus-head battle this morning. Mercury
is at the final degree of your relationship sector; don't let
anything go unsaid before he moves on. By afternoon, your
expression will be deeply intense.

Saturday 9th

Two planetary shifts occur today and these will probably have a profound effect on you. Mercury gets deeper into your intimacy sector whilst Venus glides serenely into your relationship sector. Partnerships can benefit greatly from these planetary positions. Get to know someone better by connecting on a soul level. Conversations will be unusual and risqué.

Sunday 10th

Mercury bumps into Saturn today, which should be a lesson of great importance. You're probing very deeply but you must consider someone else's boundaries. You have a shell to protect you, they may not. Be mindful that you can be over-powering. Don't spoil a good thing now.

Monday 11th

Jupiter is on hand for today's lesson. Whatever Jupiter touches gets bigger, and today he's in contact with Mercury who likes to talk. You could be asking all the right questions but getting back more than you bargained for. Do you really want to go there?

Tuesday 12th

It is possible that you will be privy to secrets or gossip today. You may be shocked at something you hear from someone you are in an intense conversation with. This could also come from your social sector. Your values will be questioned, even by yourself; you might try something new. Don't be the person to pass things on, however - just because you heard it, doesn't mean you have to spread it.

Wednesday 13th

A New Moon in your relationship sector occurs today. This is an excellent time to make goals and intentions regarding your responsibilities in partnerships. Business and romantic partnerships are both needing some kind of solid base to build upon. You're prepared to go the extra mile for this.

Thursday 14th

Uranus, the disruptor planet, turns direct today and you may feel this like a shock wave or revelation in your social sector. Ego battles are very likely and arguments may develop. Emotional triggers are being pushed. Try to pull back from probing too deep with a new person.

Friday 15th

Tension eases today but will leave you feeling flat. You may feel that you have already lost the race before starting it. Try to see the bigger picture and retreat into your shell for a while. There is always hope; you simply need to slow down or take a step back.

Saturday 16th

The Moon moves into your travel sector and, although you are more outgoing, you're prone to dreaming about the wider world. This energy can be hard to pin down but is great for making future plans. Create a vision board and write or draw everything you wish for.

Sunday 17th

Neptune and the Moon meet up today. Your heart is yearning for travel and adventure. Higher education could also be calling you. At this time of the month, it's good for you to check in with your higher self and try to find your direction. There's no harm in dreaming.

Monday 18th

You begin the working week with all systems fired up and ready to go. A sense of responsibility and commitment to your career is strong. However, you may come across some opposition or upsets from your social circle. The best-laid plans may need to be rearranged.

Tuesday 19th

The Sun enters your intimacy sector. Recent tension here can now be resolved and a fire may be rekindled. Be careful that your ego doesn't get involved and dampen that flame. You can be over-enthusiastic and forget that others have feelings too. Make your actions match your words.

Wednesday 20th

Mars the warrior planet meets up with disruptive Uranus in your social sector. This can go two ways. Group interactions can be innovative and energetic, or they can be argumentative and cause schisms. Other planetary aspects suggest that this combination of energy can produce great things. A midweek social experience could be fun.

Thursday 21st

The Moon will also meet Mars and Uranus today in your social sector, creating an interesting gathering. Whatever the energy has produced for you now, you will be emotionally involved. Elders in your groups have something to teach you. Don't take this personally, but listen to what they have to say as you will benefit from it.

Friday 22nd

Change or endings will be the themes for today. From the perspective of your social life, what needs to be lovingly transformed? You may need to let someone go now who isn't providing you with what you need. Perhaps they aren't nourishing your soul as others are. Harsh words are spoken; be kind and compassionate.

Saturday 23rd

The Moon enters your hidden sector and you get a chance to dream with a loved one. Casual conversation will be sweet and taste of the exotic delights of foreign travel. Your private mind is busy with inquiry, but you're not yet ready to speak about it with anyone. Bide your time.

Sunday 24th

The Moon meets the point of destiny today and you find that you're reaching out to the future. Your inner teacher may guide you to consider all sustainable and sensible options. You may wish to find a spiritual leader now, but you cannot settle on one train of thought.

Monday 25th

You have an unsettled and indecisive mind at work. It may be difficult for you to concentrate as your focus is scattered. This evening you should feel more like yourself as the Moon enters your sign. Soothe yourself with favourite food and come back to a grounded, centred place of peace.

Tuesday 26th

An underlying current disturbs your peace today. This may come from your social circle or possibly a health problem. Don't overdo the comfort foods, as this may be the cause. Mercury goes retrograde in a few days, so back up your devices and double-check travel plans now.

Wednesday 27th

You may be feeling more protective of yourself today. The Moon's opposition to your relationship sector highlights the demands of others. This can be a control issue if it escalates, so don't be afraid to go back into your protective shell and turn a blind eye. There's no need to get involved in other people's dramas.

Thursday 28th

A Full Moon in your finance and value sector shows you exactly where you should be putting your energy. Time to check in with your bank balance and tidy up. You may be in for a small shock, but this will trigger you to balance your spending this year.

Friday 29th

A blending of the Sun and Jupiter in your intimacy sector
brings you some luck today. Altruistic people, yourself
included, may get involved together and make something
magnificent happen. A closer, more personal relationship will
have added warmth and may reach a new level of commitment.
You're brave enough to reach out now.

Saturday 30th

This weekend, you must do some decluttering and look
after your health. It is possible that you can exhaust yourself
looking after everyone's needs today. This is a day when
running around like crazy, trying to get jobs done, is not
conducive to your wellbeing.

Sunday 31st

Mercury goes retrograde today in your intimacy sector.
This area also deals with sex, death and rebirth, or rather
endings and beginnings. Be mindful of your words as they
can be misunderstood at this time. Review your financial
situation, especially accounts you share with another. Taxes,
investments and pensions may need evaluating too.

FEBRUARY

. . . .

Monday 1st

Venus enters your intimacy sector today. As both Venus and this sector involve money, you can expect to have issues with shared finances. Venus will help to increase your sense of what is valuable to you. Ego battles from within your wider social groups are likely and can be volatile.

Tuesday 2nd

Emotional attachments to your home and family please you at the moment. There is harmony and balance. You prefer to ensure that everyone has what they need in order to tick along nicely. Today is one of those easy days where this can be achieved. The only tension you experience is outside of the family.

Wednesday 3rd

The conflict within your social groups likely concerns money. Mars and Venus are squaring off, which means that you might experience lovers' tiffs. You may not agree on how to spend money to enjoy your time with a loved one. You're determined to discover the underlying reasons why.

Thursday 4th

Your mood can be erratic today. The Moon is not making happy connections. From your sector of expression and love, you receive oppositions which can be turbulent, restrictive and aggressive right now. Neptune reminds you that surrender is not always a bad thing. Take time to look at problems from a different perspective.

Friday 5th

Mercury retrograde may catch you out today. Your emotions can be deep and mysterious, even to you, but you may find that you express them and upset someone close. It's possible to stay in control and resolve this mishap. By evening you should find yourself feeling more outgoing and optimistic.

Saturday 6th

Venus and Saturn have a cosy talk in your intimacy sector. Venus wishes to share the love and stop fighting. Saturn shows her how to do this responsibly. Great things are possible today if you remain cheerful and remember to show compassion to those around you. Shine by example today; people will notice.

Sunday 7th

Today you're inhibited by a conflict of interests. The two karmic points of the past and future are triggered, and you'll probably feel stuck in the middle. You may touch a nerve and cause a tantrum within your friendships. Stick to your guns and don't sacrifice or compromise yourself.

Monday 8th

Relationships with significant people are now in your focus. You wish to make progress with a certain person but find that you cannot communicate. Mercury is in the heart of the Sun and is saying nothing. He asks that you take your turn and listen to messages you may receive.

Tuesday 9th

Subtle manipulation from your relationship sector will make you feel uneasy today. Mars and Neptune should help you to stay controlled and empathic, whilst another may try to force their will on you. You may also be the one pulling the strings today, just mind that this does not backfire on you.

Wednesday 10th

The Moon visits your intimacy sector today. This also deals with shared finances and endings. You will feel the push and pull of all the planets here now and this may overwhelm you. Although the general mood is satisfactory, there's tension brewing around you. Don't be a people pleaser.

Thursday 11th

A New Moon in your intimacy sector gives you a chance to stop, breathe and look around you. It's possible that something has just ended whether you wanted it to or not. Grand gestures of love and romance could come your way, but you may be suspicious or fearful.

Friday 12th

As the Moon slips into dreamy Pisces, a fellow water sign, you may feel as though you are floating away in a dreamy bubble. Are you love struck? Be careful that idealistic thinking doesn't make you turn to unhealthy choices to have fun. Stay in your body and do not numb it.

. . . .

Saturday 13th

You're still unreachable today, as your thoughts are drifting miles away. A sensual or spiritual encounter has gripped you. Sexual energy can be high, but stay grounded because Mercury retrograde is with Venus, the Goddess of love. You may misunderstand another's intentions or be seduced easily.

Sunday 14th

As you land back into reality, there are things you need to see to. This could be preparation for the working week ahead or clearing up a mess. Be warned that Mercury meets Jupiter today, so any retrograde setbacks can be bigger than expected. Double-check your words, devices and travel plans.

Monday 15th

You jump into the week with all guns blazing, ready to make a difference and put your ideas out there. This makes a good impression on bosses or elders that you have to deal with in your wider community. Don't get ahead of yourself; take baby steps and don't be rushed.

Tuesday 16th

Today you can get things done and make necessary changes in the workplace. This may be challenging but, with some increased effort, you can manage it. Draw on your strengths and talents to transform outdated ways of doing something. A financial arrangement may be improved upon. You are altruistic and benevolent now.

Wednesday 17th

As the Moon dips into your social sector, you should find that
the good things in life are calling you. A shake-up is needed
and this may include evaluating friendships which no longer
align with your sense of belonging. Someone in your tribe may
be the cause of a revolutionary awakening.

Thursday 18th

The Sun is now in your travel sector. Your dreams regarding
higher education or spiritual matters may be enhanced or
given a reality check. Aggression in your social circle will leave
a bad taste in your mouth. Sweeten it with comfort foods when
you have time alone.

Friday 19th

Romantic endeavours may be thwarted today as Venus
and Mars are squaring off. Mars is in Venus' home and is
overstaying his welcome. Right now, you desire to flirt with
new ideas and unusual people, but the comforts of familiarity
leave you conflicted. Try doing something outside of your
norm for a change.

Saturday 20th

Over the weekend, your mind will be busy processing concepts
that you have not yet got to grips with. Explore all the options.
This can be uncomfortable for you, but is necessary for your
personal growth. Keep what you learn to yourself for now;
don't share until you are ready.

Sunday 21st

Mercury turns direct at last. Use today to assess any collateral damage which may have occurred recently. Emotionally, you're pulled towards a waiting future, but you don't know what that is just yet. It could be that your introspection still has more to offer. Wait and see.

Monday 22nd

The Moon enters your sign and you feel the shift as nurturing and nourishing. Your intuition is strong now, so listen to it carefully. This can feel like maternal love wrapping you in safety. Instinctively, you take care of your own needs before seeing to those of others. You are protective of yourself.

Tuesday 23rd

A little whisper from dreamy Neptune asks you to take some time with your own thoughts today. Imagination is lively and can lead you to an internal adventure, which you may want to follow up at some point. A spiritual retreat attracts, and you give this some consideration for a future trip.

Wednesday 24th

Opposition from important relationships may nag you out of your happy zone. Pluto, the planet of permanent change, rears his head and asks that you pay him some attention. What or who, from your relationship sector, needs to change? Be brave and compassionate when making this happen.

Thursday 25th

This can be a difficult day. You may experience challenges from your intimacy sector. This is also part of a necessary transformation for you. Conversations with those in charge can feel restrictive and blocked. Venus is having none of it and glides into your travel sector, ready to be the ethereal mermaid of your dreams.

Friday 26th

You could feel rebellious today and make changes in your home environment. Bold statement prints or furnishings can unleash your creativity. This evening the Moon sits opposite Venus and acts as a mirror to your desires. Research and interaction with others are needed to make holiday plans manifest for the future.

Saturday 27th

A beautiful Full Moon in your communications sector shows up anything that needs to be cleaned up or filed away for later. Details you may have missed regarding conversations will become obvious and you'll wonder how you missed them. Deal with your mind clutter and discard anything no longer useful.

Sunday 28th

A lot of grounding energy from planets in earth signs helps you stay on task today. Neptune may try and beguile you with fantasy thinking, but you'll likely resist. Keep both feet on the ground and you will get through the day having done all chores and with time to spare.

MARCH

· · · · · · · · · · · · · · · · ·

Monday 1st

An uplifting day brings a good start to the week. Your home life benefits from harmonic relationships and wisdom from family elders. Both Saturn and Jupiter are helping to keep things responsible and just. Your natural instinct to nurture your kin attracts them to you.

Tuesday 2nd

Today you know just the right thing to say and when to say it. You may be called on to mediate or settle a dispute. Your sense of family duty is admired. Mercury connects to the two karmic points and you can tell stories from your ancestors to help the young ones.

Wednesday 3rd

Self-expression can be about hot topics or the mysteries of life. It's possible that you shock a member of your social circle with your outspokenness on these subjects. A helpful nudge from Uranus shakes you out of your comfort zone and into a realm of spirituality and human connection.

Thursday 4th

Today you must watch what you are saying about your interest in the taboo. It's likely that you upset a person in authority who, in turn, belittles your opinions. Nevertheless, you are strongly drawn to the study of subjects which you haven't previously considered. A different perspective becomes useful for this.

Friday 5th

In your sector of health and duty, you wish to get all the mundane jobs out of the way and enjoy more freedom. Mars is now making enquiries into your hidden sector and discovering what makes you tick. Expect a lot of conversation with unusual groups and your intimate partner.

Saturday 6th

You're out and about today, and nothing can stop you. You are on a mission for fun. Attach yourself to people who are larger than life and have stories to tell; this is what will make you happy. Of course, it could be you being the centre of attention telling tall tales.

Sunday 7th

A sweet Sunday with a loved one or someone you have great respect for is on the agenda. When the Moon is in this sector, it is also a time to do shadow work. This will involve allowing parts of yourself that you dislike to be seen and acknowledged.

Monday 8th

Your mood turns towards caring for another. You would like to involve them in your dreams and aspirations. Uncertainty about how much you can share with this person unsettles you. A gentle discussion about a holiday to an exotic land will make you see things through their eyes.

Tuesday 9th

As the Moon meets Pluto in your relationship sector, you're likely to feel slightly manipulated. This isn't necessarily true; your own perceptions are deceiving you. A sensitive soul like you needs to take a step back and breathe. When the Moon shifts, you get a wider perspective and regain your self-assertion.

Wednesday 10th

The Sun meets Neptune today in your travel sector. This will have the effect of burning away any illusions you may have had. What may once have looked like a good plan may now turn out to be quite the opposite. As the Moon then meets Saturn and Jupiter, you get confirmation.

Thursday 11th

Your heart and head have a battle today. This will be aggravated by a poor connection to Mars, making you feel irritated. Mars in your hidden sector can add a sense of intrusion into your private life and you want to stay hidden. This can be an unsettling phase.

Friday 12th

Surprise yourself today and try to learn something new about different cultures. Watching documentaries with friends can rev you up for a trip abroad. Thinking about all that tasty exotic food whets your appetite and you get searching for a culinary experience with a difference. Where would you like to go?

Saturday 13th

Today there is a New Moon in your travel sector. Now is the perfect time to set intentions for those dreams of travel or higher education. You may set yourself on a quest equivalent to the search for the Holy Grail. Make sure it's realistic and attainable to avoid disappointment later on.

Sunday 14th

Another dreamy day is upon you as Venus and Neptune meet up. These two together will give you the most romantic, ethereal, beautiful day. You're seduced by the unusual now. Plans and goals seem more of a possibility with the combination Saturn and Mars on your side. This is your green light.

Monday 15th

The week begins with the Moon in your career sector. You are highly regarded in your career as you have confidence and can inspire people. There's a good chance that you impress those above you who will highly commend your actions. You are a leader today.

Tuesday 16th

Mercury steps into your travel sector and is eager to make plans with you. You will find that your ability to network and research comes easy now. Keep your emotions at bay today, as they will impede your hopes to transform old ideas into new. Let your head rule your heart.

Wednesday 17th

A determined Moon in your social sector will make you a little rebellious today. Do you really want to go against the flow of your friendship groups? You consider whether they are the right groups for you. Are there better groups with whom you can enhance your personal growth?

Thursday 18th

Today you may feel as if you are being selfish. As a natural nurturer, this goes against your inclinations and disturbs you. However, you clash with someone above you whilst trying to say your piece. Do what's right for you, always, but remember others have feelings too.

Friday 19th

Once again, your mind is busy processing new ideas, concepts and evaluating recent events. You ruminate wildly and get nowhere. This is because you have difficulty thinking without an emotional charge. Mars gives you the power and drive to battle through this by yourself. Saturn helps you to remember your personal boundaries.

Saturday 20th

The Spring Equinox in your work sector asks that you take a deep breath. Hold that breath before diving into the new astrological year. You will be fired up with inspiration and a new passion for your career aspirations. The Moon in your hidden sector releases a long-held dream.

Sunday 21st

Venus now follows the Sun and becomes the lady boss. Her love of wealth and harmony will work to enhance your career goals. This looks like a winning streak. Mercury and Uranus discuss possible travel opportunities with friends. You may enlarge your social circle with innovative people now.

Monday 22nd

Your sector of money and possessions get an uplift today. You are emotionally driven to spend time at home. Entertaining friends or simply chatting and touching base online can be easy and satisfactory activities to help you relax right now. You wish to feel nurtured and protected by new groups of people who share your mindset. Your tribe is calling you.

Tuesday 23rd

As the Moon and Neptune connect, you're prone to wandering off alone in your thoughts. You desire to merge with a group, but you don't fully understand what they stand for as yet. Getting in with new people may make you feel small and unworthy.

Wednesday 24th

The Moon is making a lot of connections today. Emotional instability is possible. Venus is the biggest pull as she is in the heart of the Sun in your career sector. She is powering up to be the best example she can possibly be for her colleagues. Take her advice and follow her lead.

Thursday 25th

Do you feel unworthy and undeserving of the luck you are having at the moment? Express what it is you need to grow, and it will be granted. The Sun and Venus are making things very hot, maybe you find a love-connection in the workplace. Don't be afraid to speak up today.

Friday 26th

You're duty-bound to get things done today. Find your to-do list and work through it steadily. A pleasant surprise or invitation from your social groups delights you. Mars in your hidden sector may indicate a way forward that is energetic, sexy and powerful. Use this energy wisely.

Saturday 27th

Reservations and doubts will prevent you from marching on with weekend plans. The Moon sits opposite Mercury and Neptune, causing you to discuss a lot of different angles before deciding on a course of action. Be warned, there isn't a lot of clarity when Neptune is involved.

Sunday 28th

A Full Moon in your family sector can highlight any tensions within your family. This Moon asks for balance and harmony. You may see truces and reconciliations now. Venus sits opposite and views how you deal with this. She rules this Moon and needs to see tact and diplomacy.

Monday 29th

Air energy is strong today. This is good for networking, discussions and offering up new ideas to those in charge. You will be highly regarded by authority figures. You certainly know how to make an impression today if you come out of your protective shell and speak your mind.

Tuesday 30th

To what lengths will you go to let someone know how you really feel? Nervous tension is building inside of you and it must be released. You are blessed by Mercury and Neptune, who can work together and make you the romantic, the poet and the lover. Be brave, express your feelings today.

Wednesday 31st

Your heart is pumping with intensity and you feel that it may soon burst. Where have these deep feelings come from? Verbalise your dreams, fall in love with foreign cultures and be guided by your intuition. You're responsible and respect personal boundaries. This is a lucky day.

APRIL
....

Thursday 1st

You're outgoing and optimistic today. There may be a list of
jobs to get done but this is easily achieved. Self-control helps
you get through the day with time to spare. However, this does
not mean that you relax; you have more energy to be used up
by evening.

Friday 2nd

The Moon meets the point of past karma, as it does every month.
Many other connections from your ruling luminary mean that
you can assess past actions and skills. Sun and Venus help
to keep your mood sweet as you discuss future plans with a
partner or loved one.

Saturday 3rd

A nudge from Mercury in your travel sector triggers you
into over-thinking mode. You are more sensitive today and
comments from others may touch an open wound. Put it to
one side but try to understand why this has bothered you.
Turn your attention to those people who are important to you.

Sunday 4th

The Moon is now in your relationship sector. You may not be in
the mood to deal with other people's needs today and this can
cause problems for you. Mercury is at the final degree of the
entire zodiac; mental faculties can be clouded so do not act yet.

Monday 5th

Relationships are difficult today as there is an element of control or a power struggle going on. Take a step back until the Moon passes into your intimacy sector and makes a better connection to Mercury. Communication will be easier this afternoon; someone is more willing to listen, it might even be you.

Tuesday 6th

Today you must be responsible and stay within safe boundaries. There is tension coming from your social sector, but you need not become involved. A useful connection between Venus and Mars helps to manifest what you have perceived as an impossible dream about your career progression.

Wednesday 7th

A meeting with a person you admire or can learn from lifts your spirits. Today you're driven to learn about the wider world and what you can do to make a difference. A buried dream may now find the avenue for release, it's simply a case of connecting with the right people.

Thursday 8th

The Moon slips into your travel sector and you have a deep desire to merge with a tribe of like-minded people. Spiritual matters come to mind. You must remain fluid and not fix on any one train of thought. Try before you buy into anything new and unusual now.

Friday 9th

Neptune says hello to the Moon today. New ideas about religion and spirituality need to be looked at from all angles. Neptune might trick you into a sense of security but be warned, this can be addictive and numbing. Get a reality check now, before you drift away.

Saturday 10th

You are fired up and have an action plan in mind. If you escaped Neptune's seduction, you are now on the road to making solid plans. Inspiration flows nicely and clear thinking returns to you. Saturn and Jupiter are guiding you to make better choices regarding people who lead you astray.

Sunday 11th

As the Moon meets Mercury in your career sector, you have an emotional attachment to your duties. It's possible that you have a better sense of how your personal growth will be achieved this year. If your heart is in it, then it's right for you.

Monday 12th

A New Moon meeting Venus today is a great sign that your recent discoveries are leading you in the right direction. Make intentions and goals regarding what it is you really want. How do you wish to be perceived? How can you find success by following your passion?

Tuesday 13th

Conflict can arise from within your social sector today so be prepared for it. Friends may fall away as they're not in alignment with your path now. If this happens naturally, then let them go with love. Your self-worth isn't measured by the friends you keep. Those who truly love you will still be there for you.

Wednesday 14th

Venus is at the last degree of your career sector. Before she leaves, she asks that you ensure there is harmony in the workplace. Friends you have left behind may still be around you at work. Be professional and do not bring personal problems to work with you.

Thursday 15th

As Venus skips into your social sector, she soothes the tension and becomes the party girl. Spirits are lifted and plans are made for exciting social events. You can expect a lot of indulgence in this sector now. Eating, drinking, dancing and spending lots of money is what Venus does best.

Friday 16th

Take a good look at your dreams again today. You may have a moment of crisis where you feel that they are not possible and want to give up. Sleep can be filled with anxiety. Time spent alone with your innermost hopes and wishes helps you to get things straight.

Saturday 17th

A difficult day may follow a sleepless night. Mercury, the trickster, is playing games with your mind. Surrender feels like your only option. Stick with it, this will pass as quickly as the Moon shifts. Do not make decisions or conclusions just yet as these may change again.

Sunday 18th

The Moon is in your sign and you need to self-soothe with home comforts and trustworthy people. Mercury is in the heart of the Sun; it's futile to try to get clarity now. Allow yourself to indulge in good food and downtime with a favourite book or TV show.

Monday 19th

Mercury and the Sun enter your social sector together. Venus hosts them both in her own sign. For you, this means that your wider groups, including social media, will now be filled with activity. Try to find meaningful connections with others and note what makes you feel good.

Tuesday 20th

There is a resistance coming from your relationship sector. This could be a person you are connected with or your own shadow asking to be noticed. Communications may be overwhelming, and you need to withdraw. Make yourself heard without being pushy. Find a bit of courage today to guide you.

Wednesday 21st

Blocks appear in your way wherever you turn today. Rumblings from your hidden sector may reveal things and you retreat back into your protective shell. Make sure that it's not you doing a hit and run. You must be prepared to back up what you say when confronted.

Thursday 22nd

Mars is at the final degree of your hidden sector. One last push may be needed to finalise or manifest a dream. The Moon enters your communication sector and gives an emotional charge to everything you say today. Check all the details and clear out any chaos in this area.

Friday 23rd

Venus and Uranus meet up today in your social sector. This energy has the effect of overdoing the good things in life or a big falling out with friends. Today is likely to be unstable, so don't expect things to flow easily. Mars enters your sign and helps you protect yourself.

Saturday 24th

Now Mercury meets Uranus. Gossip will be rife, and your social circle could suffer from internet trolls or a malicious infiltrator. Alternatively, if this energy is used wisely, your groups could have a lively discussion and come up with something bold and innovative. Many minds can do wonders or cause earthquakes.

Sunday 25th

Mercury and Venus connect today and have crisis talks. They both square off with Saturn in your intimacy sector. A person in charge or an elder will have something to teach you today regarding how far you push. You or others may have gone too far and caused a schism.

Monday 26th

You have the energy and drive to enjoy time with your family. Are you the harmonising factor in your family? You may be called upon to nurture or bring peace. People feel safe in your presence as they sense your protective shell and wish to share it with you.

Tuesday 27th

An intense Full Moon falls in your creative sector today. This makes difficult connections to all the planets opposite in your social sector. Total exposure cannot be avoided now. Anyone who hasn't been playing fairly will be shown in their true colours. You express your wishes loud and clear.

Wednesday 28th

Pluto, the planet of permanent change and transformation, turns retrograde in your relationship sector today. He has been there for many years, so this could feel like Groundhog Day to you. Be prepared for massive changes in this area. Self-control is paramount now; get your power back and keep hold of it.

Thursday 29th

The Moon hits a point where you turn to your past skills and experiences to help you out. This is a safety buffer that you have outgrown and need to move away from. Skills you have mastered are useful, but now is the time for new growth.

Friday 30th

The Sun meets Uranus in your social sector. This could have the effect of heating up any instability and letting off the steam needed to clear the way. You may feel this like a sense of relief. The pressure has been lifted and dissipated. Friendship circles might now feel lighter.

MAY

· · · · · · · · · · · · · · · · · ·

Saturday 1st

What next? You may sense completion but no urgency to
do anything else today. The Moon isn't making any contacts
whatsoever, although it's sitting in your relationship sector.
This could feel disappointing or peaceful, depending on your
mindset. Enjoy the break and relax a little.

Sunday 2nd

Pluto gets a visit from the Moon. He's in retrograde now and
tugging at your heartstrings. Do you wish to be in control of
your relationships, or would you prefer that they control you?
Venus and Neptune suggest that this can be a day of working
together to achieve harmony.

Monday 3rd

Your intimacy sector is touched by the Moon and you realise
that, after all the recent upheaval, you desire a closer bond
with someone special. There may be making up to do before
this can move forward. Saturn reminds you to be respectful
and adult in your behaviour.

Tuesday 4th

Mercury enters your hidden sector. He will be rooting around
in the darkest depths of your psyche, trying to find the gold
that you keep hidden. Those thoughts that keep you awake at
night will intensify. Self-reflection and introspection will be at
an all-time high. It will be worth it.

Wednesday 5th

The Moon greets Jupiter and your emotions can be more than you are comfortable with. It is no good hiding under your shell today; you must deal with those emotions and issues head-on. As the Moon shifts, you look out to the wider world to avoid confronting your emotions.

Thursday 6th

Jupiter needs your attention. If you have been searching for truth, justice and human rights, what have you overlooked? Something may return to remind you of this today. Try to see things from a different perspective. Activism may excite you but is not the place to invest too much energy.

Friday 7th

You move from a changeable mood to an assertive one today. Something clicks in your head and all may be made clear. Loving transformations are possible now. All is not lost regarding relationships, but you may have found a solution which pleases both parties. Well done.

Saturday 8th

Mercury and the Moon work together to help you be the best person you can be, today. You are inspired to lead in some way or, at the very least, show up as a good example to others. This might go against your personal energy, but you see the worth and march on regardless.

Sunday 9th

The Moon pops into your social sector just as Venus pops out of it. You're emotionally driven to spend time with your friendship groups and rekindle connections which may have been failing recently. There are still some power struggles, but you have the wisdom and know-how to deal with them.

Monday 10th

Strength drawn from Mars in your sign helps you to settle differences in a compassionate manner. This may upset a few people and you may see tantrums. Let them act out; you have done the best that you can. Stay assertive and don't let people undermine you.

Tuesday 11th

A New Moon in your social sector allows you to see that for a new beginning there had to be an ending of sorts. Those who cause constant drama can now be dismissed from your friendship groups. This is not an easy thing to do, but it is necessary.

Wednesday 12th

You are being hard on yourself today. Internally, you wrestle with recent decisions you have had to make. Yet again you are kept awake with intrusive thoughts. Let the Moon and Venus soothe you with some Goddess love and support. Let it go.

Thursday 13th

The Sun is just far enough away from Neptune for you to see through an illusion and be glad that you have discarded it. Your heart and head have a battle as Mercury wants to know the ins and outs of everything. You are not yet ready to reveal parts of yourself to him.

Friday 14th

Jupiter is now in your travel sector. He loves the depth he finds here and wants to explore the breadth too. Jupiter wants to know the entire world. You may be eager for higher education or exotic travel experiences, now. Expand your horizons and broaden your mind.

Saturday 15th

Discreetly, the Moon slips into your sign. You may not have even noticed this shift from wrestling with your demons to being at peace. Jupiter distracted you. Take that as a cue to knowing how to deal with triggers. When you're struggling inwardly, turn your attention outwards momentarily.

Sunday 16th

An energy boost from Mars helps you deal with everything today. You are being pulled towards upset from your social circle. Keep your sights on the road ahead and not what you have had to leave behind you. Neptune helps to dissolve any unnecessary attachment you may still have.

Monday 17th

If you feel that you are being manipulated, stand back and check where this is coming from. This could be coming from your own conditioning. Check in with your inner child and ask them. Venus meets the point of fate and lights up your love life and hidden sector.

Tuesday 18th

You are fiercely proud of what you have earned and built around you. Your home is not only your shell but your castle. You are defensive today and protect your environment at all costs. Your crab claws come out and build better boundaries around what you value. It's better to be safe than sorry.

Wednesday 19th

Who around you is acting like the big boss today? This isn't at work but in your interest groups. There are restrictions in your travel and higher education sector which seem to block your way. Mercury touches a nerve in your psyche and works it through with you.

Thursday 20th

The Sun shifts into your hidden sector to help Mercury see the way. You will feel more warmth and security as deep feelings emerge into the light. The monsters under your bed aren't as bad as they seem. You surprise yourself with your ability to deal with any mess today.

Friday 21st

Communications can be difficult to deal with today as there is a conflict of interests between your head and heart. The devil on your shoulder wants to play in the mud but you desire order and neatness. Wait until clarity resumes before attempting to clean up today.

Saturday 22nd

There is no clarity yet. Mercury and Neptune are squaring off, which means that Mercury is working in a sea of fog. Saturn is getting ready to turn retrograde, adding to the feeling of a heavy weight impeding progress. Discard anything you can today; make your load lighter.

Sunday 23rd

Today might feel like wading in mud. You're side-stepping around issues that need to be dealt with. The planetary energy isn't right to face things head-on. Bide your time or crawl under a rock until this mood passes. Take a day off and spend some time alone.

Monday 24th

The weekend is over and family time may have been heavy and sluggish. Now is the time to express yourself and, if you need to, have deep conversations with a loved one. The mysteries of life attract you now and provide an avenue for exploration, poetry or sweet-talking a lover.

Tuesday 25th

You can be secretive or expressive when the Moon is in your creative sector. The darker side of life gives you more food for thought and inspires you to speak out. The Moon is connecting to newly-retrograde Saturn and you may feel the first effect of this energy now.

Wednesday 26th

A Full Moon in your health and duties sector will highlight all the little jobs and tasks that you have succeeded in doing in the last six months. This is a time to be proud of yourself. Pay as much attention to your health, too; no need to burn yourself out.

Thursday 27th

Misunderstandings in your love life are due to the Moon's opposition to both Mercury and Venus in your hidden sector. Neptune may have affected this with his rose-tinted glasses and has left you in disbelief. Someone may be exposed or be seen in their true colours now. The illusion has lifted.

Friday 28th

Use today to prepare for Mercury retrograde, which begins tomorrow. This gives him more time to explore your hidden sector. This may be a bumpy ride for you and cause you some sleepless nights. Hold tight, fasten your seat belt and breathe. Back up devices and double-check travel plans, too.

Saturday 29th

As Mercury turns, he meets Venus. The planet of love and desire asks the trickster to go easy on you. The Moon makes poor connections to two of the destructive planets and relationship matters can backfire or be a non-starter. It's best that you lie low today.

Sunday 30th

You might wish to be outgoing today, but fear the consequences. Don't worry; the Moon passes quickly and today has picked up some optimism from the Sun. It's safe to step outside and be seen. This is a great example of how the Moon affects you more than most.

Monday 31st

Today is a day to go with the flow. You come up against a brick wall with your wider groups. This is a boundary you're unable to cross. Mars in your sign is working with Neptune to dissolve this and let you through. What is on the other side?

JUNE
....

Tuesday 1st

Today has great potential for manifesting your dreams. The Sun meets the point of fate in your hidden sector. This can mean that old wounds come up for healing or that your inner compass shows you which way to go now. Emotions will be deep and intense at this time.

Wednesday 2nd

Venus slips into your sign today. She will bring luck, love, harmony, and possibly a financial boost while she is here. Thinking about your wider groups or travel plans may result in a stalemate situation. Sit tight, for now, this will soon pass. Observe and assess but do not act.

Thursday 3rd

If you are feeling conflicted today, stay in your comfort zone. Others may try and rope you into their dramas. The best thing you can do is to switch off, shut the door and say, 'not today'. Cancer natives must use that protective shell and stay away from trouble.

Friday 4th

The Moon has shifted and you reconnect with your responsibilities. Your confidence is amplified by a nice connection between Moon and Sun. Be careful of Mercury retrograde today, as you are likely to follow a thread of a dream which is totally unrealistic. Venus and Jupiter may bring you financial luck.

Saturday 5th

Momentum fails you today. The planetary energy is blocking you from getting where you need to be. Mars in your sign has lost his power as he sits opposite Pluto. You may have run out of steam or experience conflict in your close relationships. There is no use pushing this.

Sunday 6th

Social activities can be joyful and finish the weekend on a high note. When Jupiter and Venus are involved, you get more than you bargained for. This can be love, food, alcohol, or a general sense of well-being. You may be tempted to overdo it, but you'll likely regret it tomorrow.

Monday 7th

Is there something you have neglected to do over the weekend? Something will re-enter your mind and you may be in a panic to sort it out. Finer details within a big picture need attention to ensure that group activities run smoothly. Make this your priority today.

Tuesday 8th

A good connection from the Moon to both Mars and Pluto helps you to realign with your personal relationships. You may have a temporary setback with a leader in your travel or higher education sector. It is difficult for you to express your wishes to someone who believes they are in charge.

Wednesday 9th

The Moon in your hidden sector makes your mind wander. You may be indecisive or have too much to think about. If you can manage to fix on one thing and envisage yourself doing it, this can help. The Moon meets the point of fate in this sector.

Thursday 10th

A New Moon in your hidden sector is the green light you have been waiting for. Now is the time to set your intentions and bring something up from your psyche to be witnessed. Mercury retrograde is also connected, so be firm and sure of what you want now.

Friday 11th

Mercury is getting new downloads today. You may find that your mind is extra busy processing new things or putting dreams into a plan. Note everything, including dreams, messages and symbols, but don't take action just yet. Mercury will reveal the best way forward for you very soon.

Saturday 12th

Mars has marched into your sector of finances, belongings and worth. If you haven't been looking after these areas, Mars will give you a boot camp training now. The Moon and Venus meet up in your sign; women are highly featured, as is self-care and nurturing. Prepare for a pamper session.

Sunday 13th

Just as you think it's safe to drift away and relax a little, you have opposition coming from your relationship sector. Who or what is trying to make changes or end something? You are feeling disturbed about this and can get angry when the Moon meets Mars later today.

Monday 14th

You want your say today. Standing up for yourself and saying 'enough!' is what you must do. The Sun melts an illusion you have been harbouring and you are left feeling disappointed. There is unrest in your social circle. Too many people are vying for a leadership role.

Tuesday 15th

Two heavyweight planets are squaring off today. Saturn and Uranus have been struggling to be friends lately. This involves your social groups and your intimate relationships. Boundaries have been crossed, making people lose their temper. You or someone close has gone too far this time. Expect a huge tantrum today.

Wednesday 16th

Are you the voice of reason now? You may be called upon for your advice or you may be dutiful and serve others today. Be careful that you are not taken for granted. Keep your wits about you and notice if you are being used. Don't be scapegoated either.

Thursday 17th

There is a more pleasant feeling coming from your friendship groups now; perhaps someone has left and there is a lighter atmosphere. You may find yourself ruminating over an idea or concept that attracts you. Keep mulling it over until you have more information, or this could be another futile project.

Friday 18th

Spending time with family may come as a welcome relief after the tension in your social life. The Moon turns your attention to your nearest and dearest now. Plan a family event or an activity you can enjoy from home. Light entertainment is what you desire for the weekend.

Saturday 19th

If it's difficult to put yourself last today. Look around you, others are putting you first. Keeping the balance and harmony within your family is easily done. This is a pleasant day and you succeed in getting the light-hearted, loving day that you wished for. Well done.

Sunday 20th

Jupiter turns retrograde today. Right now, he is in the early part of your travel and higher education sector. For the next few months, you will be asked to reconsider your thoughts about truth, justice and leadership. Religions are re-evaluated. Anything not aligned with your nature must go now.

Monday 21st

The Sun enters your sign, this is your birthday month. Happy birthday! It's also the Summer Solstice. The Moon is in your creative sector and it's possible that you express yourself deeply, but you might unintentionally hurt another's feelings. Saturn will be upset by this if you haven't been respectful of boundaries.

Tuesday 22nd

Mercury turns direct now. What has he dug up from the depths of your hidden sector? You are emotionally well and happy today with thoughts about love, change and investments running in the background. Optimism shines through you. A promising vision is lighting you up inside.

Wednesday 23rd

Venus sits opposite Pluto today. This connection occurs across your sectors of self and relationships. It can be a power struggle or a battle of wills, but can also mean that finances need to be looked at. If you can make subtle transformations, you will be onto a winner.

Thursday 24th

A Full Moon in your relationship sector will illuminate anything you have strived to complete here. What began around six months ago may now be fulfilled and, if not, then perhaps it's time to let it go. Are you bound to someone by duty or by love?

Friday 25th

Neptune, the planet of dreamers, mystics and poets, turns retrograde today. Plans for travel or higher education could become uncertain or dissolved before they have even begun. Neptune will get you to look at things from a different perspective now. You may have to surrender and go with the flow.

Saturday 26th

Venus and Pluto are once again touched by the Moon. This time, the Moon sits with Pluto in your relationship sector. You may believe that you are being manipulated or the victim of passive- aggression. Venus sits in your sign; you must remember what you're worth and practise self-care.

Sunday 27th

This is a touchy day; you feel attacked from many angles.
Check in with your finances today as there's a chance that you
may have overspent recently. Bosses or leaders cause conflict,
making you feel blocked or small. Venus exits your own sign
and now asks you to stand up for yourself.

Monday 28th

The Moon meets Jupiter, who is newly retrograde. Any
emotions felt today will be larger than average. You are
triggered to look at the wider world and your part in it.
A lingering desire to merge with the collective is haunting.
You need to learn more about spirituality.

Tuesday 29th

An emotional push and pull causes you some turmoil inside.
There are parts of you that you're not ready to reveal, yet you
desire to share with like-minded people. Would you prefer to
push this aside as fantastical thinking and get on with the
daily grind? Think carefully now.

Wednesday 30th

You continue to have a head versus heart battle. A sensitive
soul like you needs to follow the heart most of the time.
You aren't a slacker; you can allow yourself to express your
spiritual needs and still be a responsible person. Find the right
path for you. Slowly.

JULY

· · · · · · · · · · · · · · · · · ·

Thursday 1st

A fiery Moon in your career sector keeps you busy today. A helpful connection to Venus ensures that you're seen and heard in the workplace. You are a valued team player because you have the right attitude towards meeting goals and expectations. Just don't push too far with authority figures.

Friday 2nd

At the end of the week, your motivation increases. Productivity is important as you don't wish to have loose ends hanging over the weekend. Mars and Mercury make it possible for you to be emotionally invested in getting good results despite some pushing from a superior.

Saturday 3rd

This afternoon, the Moon moves into your social sector. You can kick back and relax with your friendship groups. Good food, experiences and harmony will enhance your self-worth and make you feel good. Aim to include time with a lover over the weekend, as this can be a trouble-spot if you don't.

Sunday 4th

Are you on edge today? The Moon is making poor connections to your communication sector, and there may be a rumble between friends. This shift might have come because you have expressed yourself in a way which did not serve the collective. Were you a little selfish yesterday? Are you able to patch things up before they get too big?

Monday 5th

You have a chance to make things right today. You can see things through someone else's eyes and have the grace to admit when you're in the wrong. Neptune and Pluto help but are retrograde, so go easy and don't beat yourself up about it too much.

Tuesday 6th

The Moon slips quietly into your hidden sector. This is a time when you withdraw and rely on your inner resources. Introspection is easy now and you can process recent events. Mercury ensures that you don't get washed away by Neptune, who likes to play fantasy games with you.

Wednesday 7th

If you listen very carefully to your inner voice, clarity will come to you. Venus and Mars are asking you to consider your own self-worth. Love may be on the horizon, but you must learn to love yourself first. Saturn teaches you another lesson about boundaries; this time, your own.

Thursday 8th

Your emotions check in with your mind and seem at ease now. The Moon and Mercury have met and are in agreement today. Mercury has brought something up and your heart is ready to heal it. This afternoon, the Moon slips into your own sign and you desire home comforts.

Friday 9th

Today should run without a hitch. You're the expert at looking after your own needs and knowing when something is too much for you. Intuition is high and you may even surprise yourself. New understanding about your habits and conditioning comes to you. Old habits need to die now.

Saturday 10th

A New Moon in your sign gives you the confirmation you were looking for. It's time to make intentions and goals to heal old wounds. Underneath your shell, you have a soft interior; remember to stay protected while you work on old issues that need exposure and healing.

Sunday 11th

Mercury enters your sign today. Although the Moon is your ruler, Mercury is the one you should be listening to. He brings the messages that your intuition can pick up and process in your hidden sector. Where your personal well-being is concerned, leave no stone unturned; they all have hidden pearls.

Monday 12th

The Moon is today in your sector of finances and self-worth. On her way through, she meets Venus and Mars. Today is an excellent day for communicating with a lover. Sweet talks over dinner will satisfy that craving for security and nourishment. Make every word count.

Tuesday 13th

Lovers meet up today and share a special time together. Venus and Mars are finally together. This means that you get what you desire or can at least ask for it today. Be brave, be bold and be compassionate, this alignment is too good to miss.

Wednesday 14th

Venus and Mars are still together but now the accent has changed and you are willing to serve your lover. You may also be the best person to speak to for advice today. Your attention to detail in communications means that you do not miss a trick. Someone may be glad of your help with this.

Thursday 15th

Fantasy games and illusions may pull you away from your duties today, but this is all good fun. Time spent with family can bring a sense of satisfaction and homeliness. Combine the two and get the board games out. A little family-friendly competition will make you smile.

Friday 16th

You might need to lay the law down today; Mercury in your sector of self is at odds with the Moon. Family needs and personal needs are in conflict. This will be hard for you to deal with as you wish to take care of everyone. Let someone else step up now.

Saturday 17th

Settling disputes in your home life is a skill you have. This does, however, have the effect of making you feel taken advantage of or inconvenienced. This evening the Sun sits opposite Pluto and you plainly see who is pulling strings and pushing triggers. Double-check financial obligations with a partner.

Sunday 18th

A secret may be exposed today. The Moon is in your creative sector and you feel this deeply and intensely. However, when the Moon is opposite Uranus, you must expect the unexpected. Mercury, who rules communication, and Saturn, who rules boundaries, are both involved. Prepare for a shock.

Monday 19th

Subtle manipulation is the name of the game that someone from your relationship sector is playing now. You must be strong and see through any mists that are being thrown over you. This is all very covert and you must be on guard. If you feel in danger, retreat into your shell.

Tuesday 20th

An optimistic mood comes over you and you are more outgoing. You will get through your daily tasks with ease and have energy left over. A trip to the gym or a simple health check-up will perk you up and make you feel good about yourself today.

Wednesday 21st

A fiery Moon connects to Venus and Mars, who are also in a fire sign. This is another good day for grand romantic gestures. Make this part of your routine and you will be happy to serve a lover in a way they desire. A midweek date is looking good.

Thursday 22nd

Venus glides into your communications sector and opposes Jupiter. You may be reaching out to someone who is larger than life, but you cannot connect. Frustrations have a knock-on effect in your relationships, where the Moon currently resides. This will reflect back on you, so act with integrity now.

Friday 23rd

The Sun has entered your sector of finances and worth This may be the optimum time to increase your wealth or feelings of self-worth. Don't let your ego get out of hand now, as this will backfire on you. Keep it simple, keep it focused and allow the Sun to lead the way.

Saturday 24th

Today there's a Full Moon in your intimacy sector. Look at what you have achieved in this area in the last six months What is now glaringly obvious to you? You may need to trim down your connections in this area as superficiality will not cut it anymore.

Sunday 25th

Yesterday's Moon may have rocked a boat somewhere in your social sector. Mars and Pluto are ready for war or, at the very least, permanent change. No amount of talking around a subject will help change the fact that something now needs to end. What will this be?

Monday 26th

Gentler energy from the Moon makes you desire to merge with the right people. You may turn to religion or seek spirituality to answer this need. This is a type of self-avoidance; the answer you seek is within. Keep searching and you will find it soon enough.

Tuesday 27th

Surrender your thoughts to Neptune now; he will turn them on their head and ask that you look at them differently. You may get an 'aha!' moment and wonder why you have never seen this resolution before. No matter, you have seen it now. What will you do with it?

Wednesday 28th

Jupiter returns to your intimacy sector and hangs around at the last degree. He asks that you re-evaluate your connections to leaders and spiritual teachers. You may have outgrown the need for these. Mercury flies into your finance sector. This is good news, as he is god of commerce too.

Thursday 29th

Mars appears to rule the energy today. He sits opposite Jupiter and this can mean that aggression and hostility get out of hand. There is a bossy-boots around, let it not be you. Mars then enters your communication sector and, if you aren't careful, you may initiate arguments now.

Friday 30th

Make the most of your assertive energy today. Finish outstanding jobs before the weekend comes. Stay in control of your job list and do not let distractions throw you off. This evening you'll be ready to socialise and have a good time with your friendship groups.

Saturday 31st

It's possible that you overdo the good stuff this weekend and suffer as a result. You instinctually want to taste the delights of food and wine, dancing and singing, but somewhere along the line you must know when to stop. Be responsible; listen to your head and not your desires.

AUGUST

. . . .

Sunday 1st

Once again, Mercury is in the heart of the Sun. This is your chance to listen and receive instructions. He sits opposite Saturn, which means he has a guide ensuring that he listens well. This is what you must do today. Don't be distracted by your social life.

Monday 2nd

In your hidden sector, the Moon connects to parts of your psyche that are ready for healing. This will feel uncomfortable but remember, there is no growth without pain. Poor connections to Jupiter and Mars will make this feel worse than it is. Sit tight and breathe deeply.

Tuesday 3rd

You have a restless mind as the Moon makes many connections. You may feel unworthy of the nicer things life has to offer. Let your ego die a little. Mercury is looking after you and will help your mind process this. You will know that this is the right path.

Wednesday 4th

Let yourself be nurtured today, even if that simply means cooking your favourite meal. Addictive substances will appear attractive but will only numb the very feelings you need to experience in order to heal. Your words might get the better of you today; say what you mean or say nothing.

Thursday 5th

Communication via messages or short visits may be on the agenda today. You should have the extra energy needed to get through a long list of things from your to-do list. You will make sure that everything is present and correct. Paying attention to details will pay off at a later date.

Friday 6th

Today may feel dreamlike and surreal. The Moon in your sign of self makes connections to Neptune, Venus and Uranus. This energy can bring unexpected surprises and love tokens your way. Stay in control, as this is also opposite your relationship sector where power struggles are an issue.

Saturday 7th

You have a fierce pride in what you own. Can you extend that to your sense of self-worth? You are, after all, your most treasured possession. Celebrate who you are and what you've achieved in building a home. People will flock to your nurturing soul.

Sunday 8th

Today's New Moon in your finance sector asks that you look again at what you value. You are not one for lavish items of luxury, but impulse buys can sometimes leave you feeling guilty. Make intentions now to love what you own and if you do not love it let it go.

Monday 9th

The Moon meets Mercury. You have a heart-to-heart with yourself and check in with Mercury's mission. He has rooted out all that is no longer serving you. Be brave and allow deep memories to surface and be acknowledged. Some of these may not even belong to you.

Tuesday 10th

Mars is next on the list of visits for the Moon. He is strengthening the armour of your protective shell. You may have a crisis moment today, but Mars helps you to march on. Look at how you serve others and connect with the collective. Your travel sector is ready for exploration.

Wednesday 11th

Love, desire, money and all things Venusian help to keep your heart on track today. Check your bank balance today, as you may find that you can save some money by looking at old subscriptions you no longer need. Mercury sits opposite Jupiter; you can get away with being more verbose or opinionated than usual, now.

Thursday 12th

A harmonising Moon in your family sector makes family time enjoyable. You love to entertain and have your folk around you. Mercury has just entered your communication sector which will now be a hotline of research and enquiry. Check any finances you may share with another, as they may need attention.

Friday 13th

Who is in charge in your family sector? Do you have an elder who looks after everyone's needs? This person is happy to lead but may need a little help now. Be gentle and let them think that it is their idea. Otherwise, this could bruise their ego. Alternatively, if this is you, let others help you if they reach out.

Saturday 14th

You have an odd way of expressing yourself today. Mercury and Mars can make your mind and mouth race. You may even blurt out a secret or two, or your conversations may be risqué. Saturn will pull you up on this, as you may have violated your own personal boundaries.

Sunday 15th

It's possible that, while your mouth has run away with you, you have inadvertently upset a friend. Associates from your travel and higher education sector may come down hard on you, too. Don't try to escape your responsibilities; this is your problem and you need to sort it out.

Monday 16th

Today, you might steamroller your way through your daily duties as a way to forget your problems. Your energy and your mind are racing, but you're likely to find that your heart isn't in it. The only saving grace you have today is that Venus enters your family sector and loves it here.

Tuesday 17th

You navigate the day with ease and optimism now that the tension has died down. Try to avoid being pulled off to fantastical thinking by Neptune. You should now be thinking of the bigger picture and the smaller ones within that will help you reach your goals.

Wednesday 18th

Important relationships need your attention today. Someone here is feeling neglected. Perhaps it's you who needs a hug of reassurance right now. Try to maintain a balance between family needs and those of a lover or partner. Stay joyful and hopeful and aim for peace today.

Thursday 19th

Another of the outer planets turns retrograde today. Bumpy Uranus can make an experience that topples your social sector. Mercury and Mars meet up and there can be gossip or an urgent need to offload to others. These two shifts can make today's energy unpredictable and unsettling. You will be glad to go to bed tonight.

Friday 20th

The Sun opposes retrograde Jupiter today. This can manifest as a clash of massive egos coming from your money sectors. You will be emotionally invested in the side of Jupiter who represents universal truth and wisdom. However, remember that you must observe and not act until you have made an informed assessment.

Saturday 21st

Whilst you side with the collective and become a team player, Uranus is already shaking things up in your social sector. You must evaluate these areas and see which of your friends are social acquaintances, and which are your tribe, fighting for the same causes. This is no easy task for you.

Sunday 22nd

A Full Moon on the last degree of your intimacy sector asks that you take a critical look at what it is you are standing for. It will illuminate those activities and causes that are wasting your time and energy. This Moon will also show you what excites you.

Monday 23rd

It's likely that today you will feel drained of all your energy. You have given too much of yourself recently and now need to rest and recuperate. Saturn and Venus link their influences to show you where you may have crossed boundaries not meant for you.

Tuesday 24th

Your mind is too full of head chatter today. You have every right to switch off and relax. Allow yourself to disengage from the world by watching a favourite TV show, listening to music or reading a fantasy novel. Be safe and return to Earth when you're ready.

Wednesday 25th

You are more active today and want to focus on your tasks at work. However, Mercury and Venus nag at you. There is still something that needs dealing with in the home. Bide your time, get your work done and then turn your attention towards this. You may be running around for others today.

Thursday 26th

A partner or lover may be passive-aggressive today. You have no time for this as your mind is set on your career goals. Ignoring this person will not make them go away but will help to show them they are not a priority. Use that armoured shell today.

. . . .

Friday 27th

Your mood is already turning towards having a weekend of fun with friends. Invitations come in and please you. If letting off steam is what you desire, make sure that you are safe and with trusted friends. Remember that volatile retrograde Uranus is hanging out in that sector.

Saturday 28th

Venus has a hold on Uranus today making his presence unpredictable but in a healthy way. She can make him burst with laughter and show his positive side. This can mean that your weekend get-togethers can have unexpected surprises and high points. You may even come up with a new invention now.

Sunday 29th

Nice connections from the Moon to Neptune, Pluto and Mercury can round the weekend off with style. Great conversation, changes, transformations and dreams can all be shared by your groups now. Enjoy this, as by evening you will want to spend time alone to unwind and gather your thoughts.

Monday 30th

In your hidden sector, the Moon makes her monthly visit to the point of fate. You have some idea of how you imagine your future now. Leave excess baggage behind you and learn to travel as lightly as a crab possibly can. Mercury sneaks into your family sector today.

Tuesday 31st

Do not let over-thinking drag you down today. By all means, explore all avenues for your progression but avoid the pitfalls of unnecessary anxiety. Hold on to one thought at a time if you need to, but do not obsess over it too much. There are other possibilities open to you.

SEPTEMBER

· · · · · · · · · · · · · · · · · ·

Wednesday 1st

The month begins with the Moon in your own sign. You are torn between looking after your own needs and those of others. Demands from your relationships and family sectors are difficult to ignore. Put your foot down today and look after number one.

Thursday 2nd

Communications can be fraught with tension. You don't know what to say for the best. On the one hand, you need to be firm and assertive and on the other, it's empathy and compassion which will be the best tactic. Make your chosen responses wisely with respect to the receiver.

Friday 3rd

Gentle persuasion from your close relationships is not such a bad thing. Perhaps you need to be drawn out of your shell today. With a little help from dreamy Neptune and driven Mars, you may be able to achieve a balance. Romance can be both tender and sexy under this influence.

Saturday 4th

Don't overstep boundaries today. You may be in such a good mood that you innocently forget where the borders are with certain people. This will affect your wider social groups more than close relationships. Noses may be put out of joint today, so tread carefully.

Sunday 5th

A leader, teacher or other authority figure may block your way today. Jupiter retrograding through your intimacy sector is looking for deep truth and a mentor to expand your world views. Egos can clash while the Moon is in opposition to him. Don't take it too personally; observe and make mental notes.

Monday 6th

Efficient communication is necessary today. Be on the ball and pick up any errors before they turn into disasters. A misspelt message can be a trigger for unrest in your relationships. Double-check everything before hitting 'send'. Family and lovers may clash or vie for your attention today.

Tuesday 7th

A New Moon in your communication sector gives you a starting point to renew personal contracts with others. You can now decide how much you are prepared to do for others willingly. Set your own limits now. Your assertiveness might offend someone, but this is not your problem. Stand up for yourself.

Wednesday 8th

Your daily routine ticks along nicely today as the Moon is visiting your family sector. A helpful connection to Saturn in retrograde means that everyone knows their place and their duties. No-one gets over-loaded today, especially not you. Make this something that you mean to continue, lighten your load.

Thursday 9th

Mercury in your family sector is trying to say something.
Speaking from the heart to your family members may help
resolve an ongoing dispute. Tell them how you feel. Be honest
and measured with your responses. Get it all out now and you
may be surprised by the support you receive.

Friday 10th

Venus sits at the final degree of your family sector. The Moon
meets up with her and they have a discussion on women's
rights. Mother figures or strong females will feature highly
today. Women's intuition is strong, as is yours. Tune in to this
feminine wisdom now.

Saturday 11th

In your creative sector, an intense Moon brings out the
melancholic in you. Your deeper, darker side is expressed
easily. A connection to Neptune helps to make this energy
great for writing, drawing, sending letters or expressing your
deepest feelings. Venus is the muse you have been looking for.
Let her seduce you.

Sunday 12th

This morning, you may not find the energy or cheer that you
feel you need in order to get on with the day. This will change
by the afternoon when you are more outgoing and easily catch
up on the jobs that need doing. Simply work through your task
list today, breaking it down into smaller, more manageable
chunks if it's easier.

. . . .

Monday 13th

You're fired up to begin the working week. Background dreams or yearnings for higher education and travel might nag at you. These are easily ignored as you trek through the day. Conversations with family members or discussions about house rules are productive. You should find that everyone pulls their weight.

Tuesday 14th

The Sun is opposite Neptune today. Expect illusions or unrealistic goals to evaporate now. Travel plans may receive a blow as you realise you must delay or postpone a plan you have been excited about. Mars at the final degree does not help you here. You may get angry and sulk.

Wednesday 15th

Your personal, romantic relationships help to soothe your bad temper. You may get a nice surprise from someone who is trying to cheer you up. Do not take your mood out on someone who is not responsible for triggering it. Mars now becomes the mediator in your family sector.

Thursday 16th

You're feeling hurt or victimised. Stay inside your shell and lick your wounds. This afternoon, you'll feel justified or rebellious and come out again with a bang. You wish to let everyone know how you felt, that you are OK, and you love them all.

Friday 17th

Today is unlikely to go swimmingly. You clash with others in many areas. An elder or authority figure blocks your way and a sexy, seductive Venus in your creative sector may play hard to get. At the same time, unrest from your social groups causes other problems. Watch for fallout today.

Saturday 18th

You may be looking to start a revolution today. Is this really you? This is a knee-jerk reaction to something that has hurt your inner child. The Moon meets Jupiter and you need to assess your standing on group adventures. Perhaps they are no longer for you.

Sunday 19th

You have tried swimming with the collective and have come across bigger crabs than you. Today you must take an objective look at any spiritual groups you have become attached to. Have they seduced you into something that goes against your nature? Have you waded too deeply into something weird and wonderful?

Monday 20th

A beautiful Full Moon will show you exactly what has been going on with spiritual matters. It's time to sacrifice, surrender or stand up for yourself now. Have you been chasing an impossible dream? Take off the rose-tinted spectacles and take a very good look at where you stand.

Tuesday 21st

Your mental energy gets a boost from Mars sitting opposite the Moon. This could feel draining unless you work it to your advantage. You have a lot of new ideas, concepts and goals you would like to research. These may draw you to a possible future, but you must take action.

Wednesday 22nd

The Autumn Equinox today gives you a chance to be still. This energy is great to connect to when your mind is racing. Outside demands from partners and family will make this difficult for you. Try to get away and be alone for at least a short while today.

Thursday 23rd

Pangs of guilt surface within you but there is no need for this. You have divided loyalties between career and home life at the moment. Do the responsible things first, then everything else later. This afternoon you are more grounded and wish for home comforts or fun with friends.

Friday 24th

Venus sits opposite Uranus today. This can be tantalising, shocking and naughty like a Burlesque show. The deepest, seductive side of you is being expressed and you may surprise someone, even yourself. Revel in it. Be exotic, erotic and as shocking as you like. You deserve some fun today.

Saturday 25th

You may now have had a taste of the taboo and an addiction begins. Remember that this can be your shadow side being expressed. Pluto is witnessing your transformation from your relationship sector. Might this be the hidden gems Mercury was looking for earlier this year?

Sunday 26th

Mercury goes retrograde today. This time it will be in your family sector. The usual advice applies; back up all devices, double-check travel plans and be mindful of how you communicate. The Moon in your hidden sector is collecting extra emotional energy for this. Mars the warrior and Saturn the teacher are with you.

Monday 27th

Today may feel like the calm before the storm. Neptune is squaring off with the Moon in your hidden sector and giving you a chance to see things from all angles. Don't sacrifice any of your dreams right now; hold on to them tightly but view them objectively.

Tuesday 28th

The best thing you can do today is to lie low. Your mind is doing overtime and you are giving yourself anxiety. You have been overthinking and now you cannot think clearly at all. The Moon is connecting to Mercury in retrograde, so wait until it passes this evening.

Wednesday 29th

The Moon has landed gently in your sign allowing you to tend to your own needs. You may be conflicted and feel that you ought to be doing things for the family. Let Venus and Neptune help you to express yourself with pure poetry. Neptune reminds you not to sacrifice or compromise yourself.

Thursday 30th

A beautiful connection between the Moon, Venus and Neptune, floods your senses with emotional well-being. Pluto is also opposite the Moon now and you may be seduced by a lover or partner. You are drunk with love or otherwise not in this world today. Have fun while you are away.

OCTOBER

. . . .

Friday 1st

In your money and value sector, the Moon asks that you
check in with your bank balance. Is it all as it should be?
An opposition to teacher Saturn may suggest that you have
stretched the budget too far. You may very well see trouble
within your relationships today.

Saturday 2nd

What's yours is yours, isn't it? You're fiercely proud of all that
you've acquired. Your social sector invites you for an evening
out, but be careful not to overdo it. Gentle persuasion or
passive-aggression will come from your love and romance
sectors today but is harmless.

Sunday 3rd

This morning the Moon dips into your communications
sector and squares off with the points of karma and fate. What
troubles you now will seem larger than it is. This is due to
Mercury connecting to Jupiter, both in retrograde, and asking
you to re-evaluate how you behave in groups and families.

Monday 4th

Is it possible that you're not ready to begin another week? You
are drawn to being productive and getting things done but
Neptune is trying to distract you. Your dreams and plans for
future travel are on your mind. An innovative idea concerning
friendships will come to you.

Tuesday 5th

Something is asking to be changed and today you know exactly how to do it. You are methodical and practical about making a transformation of some kind. This may be your close love relationships but could also concern your finances, particularly those you share with another. Dig deep and find out.

Wednesday 6th

The planetary energy is buzzing. A New Moon helps you to make new rules in your family dealings. Moon and Sun are both there with Mars making this time action-packed and assertive. The Moon then meets retrograde Mercury. On top of that, Pluto also turns direct.

Thursday 7th

Venus has had enough of seducing you and is looking for adventure in your daily duties. She also asks that you check in with your health and look after yourself better. This afternoon you can be moody and intense. Pluto needs you to make a permanent ending.

Friday 8th

Today's energy is highly charged, so be careful. The Sun is hanging around with Mars and things could get very hot. Your family sector may be extra busy or tempers may be flaring from all angles. An intense Moon sits opposite Uranus; prepare for highly volatile encounters.

Saturday 9th

Attending to mundane chores may be the best thing you can do today. Mercury meets Mars and the Sun in your family sector. Battles of ego will test your patience. Be like Mercury and say nothing. Turn your back and let them get on with it. Women will win the day.

Sunday 10th

Saturn turns direct today and reminds you that if you didn't learn a thing or two this year, it will come back around another time. An optimistic Moon connects to Saturn, Mars, Mercury and the Sun. You're emotionally charged to settle things in your family today.

Monday 11th

Work through your job list today but don't overtax yourself. Check in with your health. You may need some immune support right now. Get that shell of yours ready for the winter. This evening your loved one is calling and a cosy night for two beckons. If single, spoil yourself.

Tuesday 12th

Business or romantic relationships demand your time and energy. Pleasant surprises or new ways of relating lift your spirits. It is possible that you see something now that was always there but out of your vision. This can excite you; you have a new toy to play with.

Wednesday 13th

The Moon meets Pluto retrograde today. This can bring unsettling feelings which you cannot pinpoint. Watch out for subtle manipulation. Your sensitive soul will perceive this as victimisation but it may be that something is changing against your will. Resistance will not get you anywhere; this needs to happen.

Thursday 14th

In your intimacy sector, the Moon meets Saturn. You will have a long discussion with an elder, or with yourself about where you have been restricted this year. The rebel inside you will surface but you manage to keep it under control. However, this will keep bubbling for a short while.

Friday 15th

Today is more optimistic. Both the Sun and Jupiter come out to play and warm your heart. You may have renewed hope in your wider groups. Jupiter is soon to go direct and you are already feeling the joy return. Emotions and ego are in sync and stable.

Saturday 16th

This weekend, your mood turns towards connecting effortlessly with others. You may find yourself engaging in spiritual activities or simply reading about them. This reignites your urge to travel and explore exotic lands. What new Holy Grail will you be chasing now? Is it the thrill of the quest that excites you more?

Sunday 17th

Venus and Mercury have a talk about exploring the truth in family situations. Somebody is not being fair. You may still feel confused today and require some downtime to switch off. Look closely at your health today, as it's likely that you're feeling drained. Avoid self-medicating with dubious substances. Get some sleep instead.

Monday 18th

You feel the shift of both Jupiter and Mercury turning direct.
Now is the time to pause, reflect and then attempt any
salvaging of recent upsetting situations. Mars boosts your
energy to do this, but don't run before you can walk. Rest first.

Tuesday 19th

A fiery Moon in your career sector helps you to navigate the
day with confidence. The Moon opposes Mercury and could
mean that your attention is required at work and in the home.
You have the energy to get all the jobs done, but don't take on
any extras. Enough is enough today.

Wednesday 20th

A Full Moon builds in your career sector. Your efforts will
now be recognised and you may have completed projects to
celebrate. This has felt like climbing an endless mountain but
you are now at the top. Celebrate success and decide on a way
forward from here.

Thursday 21st

From within your social sector, unrest bubbles. This isn't a bad
thing, it's the rumblings of something new and exciting. Your
groups are changing. You no longer need to hang out with
those who don't bring you joy. You're more inclined to make
friendships with those you can learn from.

Friday 22nd

Mars in your family sector is squaring off with Pluto retrograde
in your relationships sector. You will need to find a way to
balance the demands coming from these areas. It's tempting
to switch off and have alone time but this needs dealing with
before the weekend begins.

Saturday 23rd

The Sun now moves into your sector of creativity, passion and romance. This can be a fun time if you let it. Your inner child wants to laugh and play. You have many niggling trains of thought over the weekend and this may bother you. Forget them, go and play.

Sunday 24th

You should find a way to relax today. The Moon in your hidden sector is causing agitation from a place deep inside of you. This can cause problems with your health if you aren't careful. Getting outside and working steadily through chores will help. Talk to a close friend or to your shadow.

Monday 25th

You're gifted with joy from Jupiter and energy from Mars, yet Neptune is coercing you into a fantasy land where you can be alone with your thoughts. Be active today, even if that's just chatting to people on social media. Get involved and perhaps you can laugh a little today.

Tuesday 26th

The Moon is now in your sign. A good connection from the Sun helps you express your needs and desires now. This can be deep and intense. Someone special may witness this and a new level of understanding grows between you. Comfort foods will ease that ache to be nurtured.

Wednesday 27th

A battle between your heart and head is possible today. This will involve your close relationships where you may feel that there is no growth happening. Pause for a while and re-evaluate the worth of something if it is getting you down. Say no to what drains you.

Thursday 28th

Your pride is likely to kick in today. You're feeling irritable and protective of your self and what you've built around you. Venus and Jupiter make a nice connection in your duties and intimacy sectors. What you do for others does not go unrecognised today. You know who your true friends are.

Friday 29th

What is it that you value the most? Your home, bank balance and self-worth are all tied up with status today. A member from your social group may cause friction, but it's unlikely that you'll be slow to tell them. Discussing problems with family will help you now.

Saturday 30th

Mars enters your creative sector today. Your passion rises and you are driven to get things done to a high standard. Romantic liaisons will now be amped up by Mars in his own sign and looking for action. Do your research on a potential lover. Find out what makes them tick.

Sunday 31st

Conversations can be lusty today. Why not treat a lover to a tasty meal or a sensual experience. The intense Sun wants to rock your boat a little. Romance is strongly favoured if you play your cards right and be the best version of yourself now. Enjoy it.

NOVEMBER

....

Monday 1st

There are moments today when you want to pack it all in
and have some alone time. These are thankfully brief and
you resist. Obligations to your close relationships are filled,
keeping you in control of any changes you may have made.
Happy chatter with family elders goes well.

Tuesday 2nd

Something has gone wrong in your personal relationships and
this needs to be discussed, possibly with mediation or a third
party. Today, you aim to get justice and fairness. Getting your
point across can be tricky. Saturn will help if you remember to
give thoughtful, considered responses and not to react hastily.

Wednesday 3rd

The Moon meets Mercury in your family sector. Many thoughts
run through your head and you have an emotionally charged
decision to make. Your heart is torn as this decision needs to
be made with logic and rational thought. Make your case with
compassion, but avoid sentimentality.

Thursday 4th

A New Moon in your creative sector asks you to start anew
or seek refreshment in romantic relationships or creative
projects. The energy surrounding this Moon is touchy. Mars
gets involved and makes you irritable and maybe even angry
Uranus is also linked and this can mean disruption. Venus tries
to help by skipping into your relationship sector.

Friday 5th

A deeply emotional Moon makes challenging connections today. There is no point holding on to something if it no longer serves you. If you cannot transform it for the better, let it go. Mercury enters your creative sector and will do some depth psychology on these issues.

Saturday 6th

The Moon hits the point of the karmic past. This confirms the need to move on from a challenging situation. Whilst Mercury tries to help Venus out and discover what the real issue is, Saturn asks that you be adult about it. Distract yourself with mundane duties for now.

Sunday 7th

Neptune is attempting to dissolve a belief you hold dear. You aren't ready for this and concern yourself with being busy and connecting to wider groups. You put energy into the wrong places and, by the end of the day, may feel guilty about this. Try not to burn out.

Monday 8th

The Moon enters your relationship sector and makes helpful connections to most planets. There is a way to resolve your troubles. The Moon and Venus make you more sensitive, compassionate and determined to make things work. Mars and Mercury at the beginning of your creative sector are helping you commit to this.

Tuesday 9th

You now look at things through the eyes of another. Where might you have projected your ideals onto someone else? Which part of your shadow is being illuminated now? It may be that your hidden parts are responsible for any unrest in your close relationships now.

Wednesday 10th

Your rebellious streak may come out today. You find it hard to own your part in recent tension. Mercury and Mars meet and square off with Saturn and the Moon. The shell that you carry now protects your ego, but this may also have adverse effects. Hiding and sulking will only make matters worse.

Thursday 11th

Trying to justify yourself without apology leads to more unrest. Your social groups are now suffering and you may clash with someone who is bigger or more important than you. The current mood you are in is affecting all areas of your life. What can you do to resolve this?

Friday 12th

Today you take a long, hard look at where you have been responsible for upsetting people. Your shell softens and you begin to see another's point of view. Some fog should clear around these issues, making you able to see where you have been reluctant to apologise or conform.

. . . .

Saturday 13th

A lovely, gentle Moon in your travel sector helps you to see the bigger picture. Spending the remainder of the weekend re-connecting with people is your priority. The Moon sits with Neptune and dissolves your anger, although Mercury has discovered something which may startle you. Is this the beginning of self-realisation?

Sunday 14th

Enjoy today, as there is better energy for you to relax and get back into balance with yourself. Connecting with others and discussing dreams, spirituality or travel will help you greatly. This will fire you up for the week to come. The positive side of change is becoming clear to you now.

Monday 15th

Just as you think you have things in control, outside influences come to unsettle you again. The Sun and Jupiter are clashing, as are the Moon and Venus. Your ego has likely been bashed again and you're begrudging trying to make amends. Sit tight and breathe deeply.

Tuesday 16th

Today you could solve this troublesome issue. Pluto, who resides in your relationship sector, is getting connections from both Sun and Moon today. You must try not to be led by your emotions or take things personally. The Sun will strengthen your resolve and give you strength and compassion for yourself.

Wednesday 17th

As the Moon shifts into your social sector, your attention turns towards friends. It's likely that you want to let off steam today or rant and rave. Your closest friends or even your online ones are willing to let you do this within a safe environment.

Thursday 18th

Is there a way that you can get creative with all this pent up angst inside you? Mars and Mercury in your creative sector are the perfect allies for getting things out of your system and out into the world. Writing, messy painting or a harsh session at the gym will help.

Friday 19th

A Full Moon in your social sector is the valve you have been waiting to open. This is the completion of a six-month phase or a realisation that something needs to go. Venus and Uranus are there to make a gentle, loving shift if need be.

Saturday 20th

Your mind will be extra busy now as the Moon is in your hidden sector. Intrusive thoughts still keep you awake at night, but this should be when you are more open to evaluating and processing them. Try not to dismiss any ideas you may have; note them all down and review objectively.

Sunday 21st

Another day of thoughtful inquiry is necessary today. You are slowly coming to terms with the recent upheavals. You desire to switch off and enjoy some downtime, but be careful not to do this by resorting to unhealthy coping mechanisms. These will only take you back to a place of muddy waters.

Monday 22nd

You begin the week settled, but still sensitive. The Moon is now in your sign and you find that your intuition is strong. Venus and Mars connect well, making it possible to enjoy a pleasant time with a loved one. The Sun moves into your health and duties sector.

Tuesday 23rd

Today, you have a need to take care of yourself and also meet the needs of a close relationship. Home comforts and good food may be the way forward. You are learning to put boundaries in place which will benefit the people on either side. Meeting in the middle does you good.

Wednesday 24th

You may have a moment when you are over-sensitive today. It is possible that you revert back to negative thinking. This afternoon, the Moon shifts and you smile again. Courage comes back to you and you should feel proud that you resisted the temptation to negate all your good self-work

Thursday 25th

Mercury has left your creative sector now. Did you notice all that mental activity when he was there? He now sits on the point of past karma and asks you to release the baggage before moving on. The winged messenger wishes you to fly unencumbered as he does. It's time to let things go.

Friday 26th

The Moon in your sector of value is making you see that your own self-worth is part of the problem. You undervalue yourself. Why do you think you are not good enough? A spiritual leader or person in authority is also trying to make you aware of this.

Saturday 27th

Despite all the self-analysis, you still doubt yourself. Have conversations with people close to you about this. In this case, siblings would be the best ones to talk to. You will realise how much you are loved, depended on and looked up to, simply because you are a sensitive soul.

Sunday 28th

Today you ponder the concepts of sacrifice and surrender. Do you do things for others because it is expected of you? Does this wear you down? Is this the reason for your poor self image? If you're happy to serve others and you're rewarded, then it's no sacrifice.

Monday 29th

Family issues may require your attention and you're happy about this. The Moon makes great connections for networking and being your true self. Mercury has nothing to say today. You must listen and observe. Your energy is deep and intense. What will you learn today?

Tuesday 30th

Managing your family and personal relationships is not as easy, today. You may have to make promises to appease someone. Mercury and Saturn are talking about how you relate and behave in large groups. What is your role in the collective? Are you inspired to make a difference in the world?

DECEMBER

. . . .

Wednesday 1st

Exciting possibilities come back to you this afternoon. Neptune turns direct and, finally, the fog clears. He has been sitting in your travel sector, causing illusions and trying to drag you away to fantasy land. Now those dreams of exploring new cultures or exotic religions should move forward again.

Thursday 2nd

Intense discussions with a loved one provide food for thought. A shared dream or wish can add fuel to your life together. Thrashing through ideas for travel or an unusual work vacation can be something which helps the two of you bond. How far are you willing to go together?

Friday 3rd

The Moon meets Mars and you are unstoppable in your passions. Perhaps you have found the very outlet that will motivate you in love and in your personal development. This afternoon, you're already making lists and ticking things off. You're fired up from following a new direction.

Saturday 4th

A New Moon occurs in your health and duties sector. This is fortunate, as it has coincided with your plans to do something memorable. Mercury will help you do all the research now, as he sits with the Moon and enjoys taking a leadership role. Be careful to keep it real and manageable.

Sunday 5th

Your ideas and plans to get away, visit new lands or explore different cultures are getting huge now. Jupiter is linking to the Moon and expanding everything; your optimism, motivation and itinerary. Seeking the truth from around the wider world is what Jupiter wishes for you. Live it large.

Monday 6th

The Moon is now in your relationship sector and you are firmly resolute in your decision to do something exciting with a partner. You will take all the required steps to make this a real project. New plans are coming to you all the time. Start saving your pennies.

Tuesday 7th

Today you must take a good look at the finances required to bring your plan to manifestation. The Moon meets Pluto in your relationship sector and asks that you look at how joint finances can work to realise your shared dream. Explore every avenue possible now, before committing to one.

Wednesday 8th

A blockage or restriction is likely to stop you in your tracks today. This will be relatively minor, but enough to spoil your buoyant mood. Saturn wants to teach you something about acting too quickly. Find a person who has more knowledge and experience than you. Learn about possible pitfalls.

Thursday 9th

Don't run before you can walk. You're treading on new territory and you aren't the expert on it. Like a crab, side-step around this new ground and observe it before you head into it. Be armed with knowledge, and then you can gain wisdom.

Friday 10th

The Moon is now in your travel sector. Spend the weekend doing research by watching TV documentaries, reading books and looking at maps. You desire to merge with the collective and be a part of something special. Taking time to plan a short retreat may do you good and put you in the right mindset.

Saturday 11th

Venus and Pluto meet today in your relationship sector. This influence can be manipulative as both planets are connected to money. Venus needs you to remember what you've learned about your self-worth. Make sure that you and another person are on an equal footing in status and finances.

Sunday 12th

Your mind is so full of ideas that you can hardly contain them all. You need to decide which ones are 'pie in the sky' and which ones you can easily manage. The Sun is trying to help you expand your vision and not be blind-sided by illusions again.

Monday 13th

Mercury enters your relationship sector at the same time as Mars enters your health and duties sector. These shifts by inner planets will be more personal to you and you should take note. Let Mercury enhance your communication and Mars give you the energy for all the jobs you must do.

Tuesday 14th

Today you're more outwardly social and wish to connect with your wider groups. These can include online groups of people with the same interests as you. Conversations with friends can be lively and informative. Enjoy some luxury now; a tasty dinner or fine wine will suffice. You deserve it.

Wednesday 15th

The Moon meets Uranus today. The great disruptor can cause arguments to occur in your social circle, but can also cause the sort of friction which produces a pearl. You may find that your friendship groups come up with a valuable gem for you to take away and peruse.

Thursday 16th

Make the most of the Moon in your social sector. You will receive many benefits from these groups today. Neptune, Pluto and Venus connect, making this a dreamy time where you may be able to involve your lover. If single, love may come from these groups now.

Friday 17th

Mars is pumping the iron in your health and duties sector, he has his eye on the ball at all times. Unfortunately, your Mars-flavoured focus is opposed by the Moon in your hidden sector. Your mind will wander now. It will be hard to get back on track while the Moon is here.

Saturday 18th

The festive activities may ha...
planet of love, harmony, be...
This will happen in your...
may be wonky as you ...
from the distant past m...

Sunday 19th

Anxiety may get th...
hidden sec... or ca...
exposed. ...
insight into ju... you...
you awake at thi...
di...

Monday

To...
a...

DAILY FORECASTS

Sunday 26th

Women's intuit...
aggression go...
the one who ...
with a loved ...
the mood a...

Monday

You ha...
to go ...
today ...
you ...
thi...
di...